Saoirse

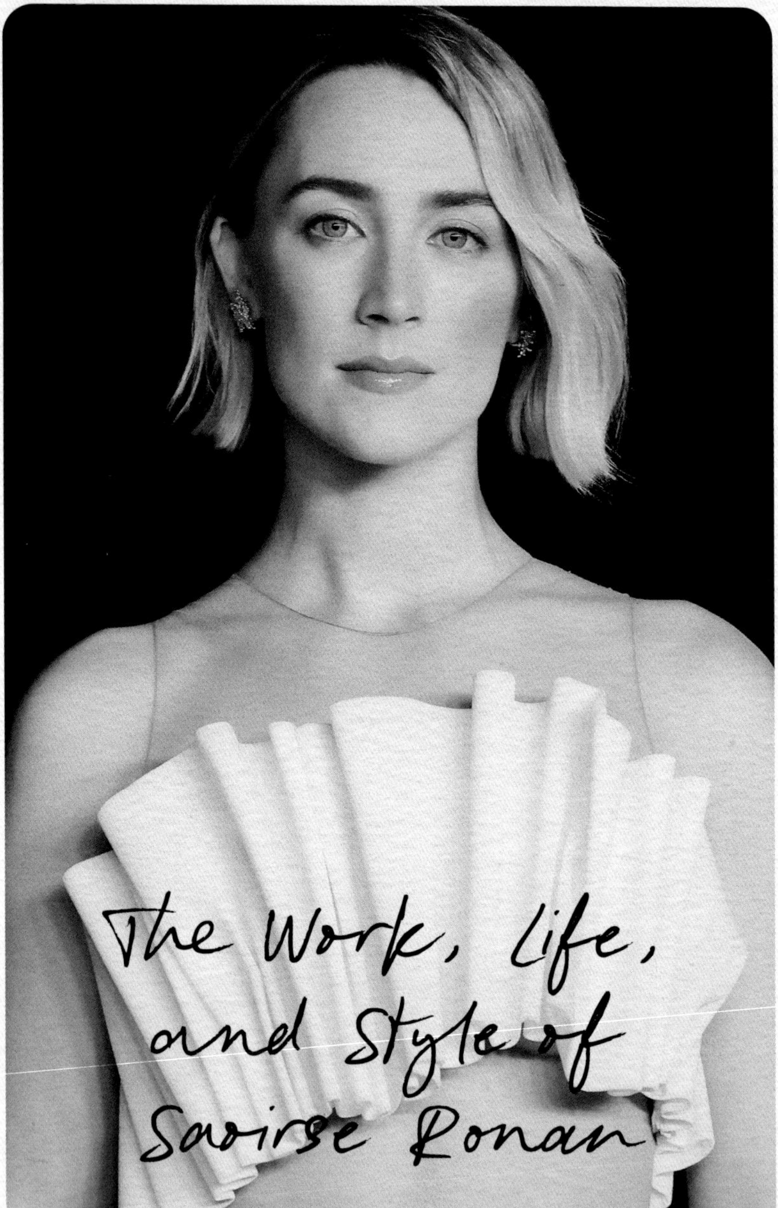
The Work, Life,
and Style of
Saoirse Ronan

Saoirse

Kaila Hale-Stern

EPIC INK

Previous: Saoirse at the third Academy Museum Gala, December 2023.

Saoirse at the fourth Academy Museum Gala, October 2024.

Contents

Introduction

The Silence That Spoke Volumes

"It felt very similar to when I am at a dinner with a bunch of my friends, and I will always make the point that, well, this is actually an experience that we go through every single day, one hundred percent."

—Saoirse on *The Ryan Tubridy Show*

Saoirse Ronan didn't expect to go viral that night. She was an old hand at appearing on *The Graham Norton Show*, swapping stories with the host and his customary panel of guests. It should have been a publicity stop like any other, like the hundreds that came before in the two decades she has spent in the Hollywood spotlight.

Yet a singular moment from the October 28, 2024 episode of *Norton* left the confines of entertainment television and rocketed around the globe. It was shared countless times across social media platforms and racked up scores of views and comments, generating international headlines in the process. All because Saoirse chose to speak up and share a perspective that left the people around her speechless.

Saoirse at Sundance Film Festival, January 2024.

To understand how the moment unfolded, the stage must be set. Graham Norton is a popular Irish comedian, actor, and TV presenter known for his irreverent interview programs. Unlike American late-night vehicles, which tend to focus on the host and a featured guest, Norton invites several famous guests on at once and cultivates a dialogue between them. His trademark is creating a rollicking, free-wheeling atmosphere, and he is an expert at producing memorable moments. The conversations can be witty, raunchy, and altogether raucous, breaking the staid model of celebrity interviews and moving them into more unbridled territory. It's not new for a clip of outrageous or hilarious commentary to make the viral rounds from *Norton*. But viewers witnessed something unexpected when Saoirse sat on the couch this time—something that caused her segment to break out for a different reason.

For the October taping, Saoirse was bookended on Norton's red couch by three male movie stars. Like her, they were some of the most respected actors in the business. There were two leads from *Gladiator II*: the legendary Denzel Washington and Paul Mescal, who was also Saoirse's *Foe* costar, friend, and fellow young Irish actor risen to top-billed cinematic prominence. On her other side sat Eddie Redmayne, recently off his Broadway *Cabaret* run and now playing an infamous assassin in a TV reboot of *The Day of the Jackal*. Slotted between the more casually attired men, Saoirse was the picture of elegance in a black one-shouldered dress, her dark blonde hair twisted into a sleek bun. She was there in part to promote her role in director Steve McQueen's *Blitz*, where she plays a young mother separated from her child in World War II–besieged Britain.

Much of the show proceeded in the accustomed manner, with laughs, jokes, and prompts from Norton that guided the guests to discuss their projects. Redmayne spoke about the intense training he underwent for his thriller TV series. As his character is in constant danger, he had to learn how to fight back with whatever was at hand. One such everyday item that the military production advisor showed him how to use as a defensive weapon was his phone.

This elicited an amused response from the men on the couch. Mescal laughed and said, "Who is actually going to think about that? If someone actually attacked me, I'm not going to go, 'phone.'" Norton joined in on the "fun," pretending that he was on his phone and then came under attack. He joked that he would tell the assailant, "Can you hold on a second?" Redmayne agreed with them: "That's a very good point." It's clear that beyond training for a violently dramatic role, no scenario had prompted these gentlemen to consider grabbing an everyday object for self-defense purposes. The idea of it was treated as outlandish.

As the banter went back and forth, you could see that Saoirse wanted to speak—she tried to say something, but the jokes rolled on, and she couldn't get a word in. A few seconds later, now determined, Saoirse did interject.

"That's what girls have to think about all the time," she said.

Just ten words, and those around her were struck silent. "The look on the other actors' faces after Saoirse has detonated this chat-icide bomb is hilariously mesmerizing," noted *The Guardian*, "as is the

(left to right) Denzel Washington, Paul Mescal, Saoirse Ronan, and Eddie Redmayne during filming for *The Graham Norton Show*, London, October 2024.

sudden silence, which is split-second but also seems to last twenty-seven years." Saoirse then turned to the audience for confirmation—"Am I right, ladies?"—and was met with loud applause. In describing the immediate aftermath, *New York Magazine*'s *The Cut* wrote, "As the men laughed in discomfort, she threw up a double 'hang loose' sign, which I am interpreting here to mean, 'We can all agree I just absolutely owned these rich boys.'" While she did absolutely inhabit the moment and transform it, Saoirse was making a much more salient point, one that had nothing to do with one-upmanship.

"That's what girls have to think about all the time."

If Saoirse hadn't been on the couch, and if she hadn't been willing to provide a much-needed reality check from the female perspective, this exchange between the men on *Norton* would likely have gone unnoticed. Just another story about actors learning an unorthodox skill for a role and some levity about it. But Saoirse *was* there, and she did speak up. In the process, she got the whole world talking.

"Thank you for saying what all women were thinking," read one typical TikTok response on a shared clip of the *Norton* segment. "The silence was so loud," wrote another TikTok commenter. On X, reactions praised Saoirse in a similar vein. "Saoirse Ronan is a queen. Men need a reminder what it's like being a woman so they can appreciate their privilege," a user pointed out. "The silence after she said that spoke volumes." Another X post shared the clip with a simple caption: "that's mother," using the internet slang meaning of the word, which implies that a woman is iconic, legendary, and powerful.

Columnists and news anchors also echoed the sentiment. "No one is suggesting that the male actors and presenter involved deserve some huge backlash for this," *The Guardian* explained. "What people are saying is that the moment was telling. When clips like this go viral, it's for a reason. For this many civilians to share them—this many female civilians, let's face it—means they instantly saw something they recognized . . . For the right words to be found in the moment, on primetime television, is a fantasy arguably more powerful than any of the ones the chaps are currently promoting in their movies and prestige TV projects." And because Saoirse found the right words, at the right time, and drew such wide-ranging attention to it, this crucial discussion continued far beyond the bounds of Norton's chat show.

"Men, even the good guys, seem to have a blind spot when it comes to women's lived reality," *The Guardian* wrote in another article, highlighting that those online commenters thought Saoirse "absolutely nailed it." Paul Biddiss, the military production advisor behind Redmayne's phone anecdote, also weighed in with *The Guardian*. "Saoirse was absolutely right," he said. "As Saoirse said then, phones, along with everything else inside a handbag, are always on the mind of a woman who is walking alone."

Saoirse's interjection continued to have a profound ripple effect, bringing awareness where it was previously lacking. This included

Paul Mescal and Saoirse Ronan in *Foe*, 2023.

those who shared the couch with her on *The Graham Norton Show*. "Saoirse was spot on, hit the nail on the head," Paul Mescal said in a subsequent appearance on RTE's *The Late Late Show*. "And it's also good that messages like that are gaining traction, like that's a conversation that we should absolutely be having on a daily basis." Speaking about Saoirse, Mescal added that she is "quite often the most intelligent person in the room."

Saoirse herself was caught off-guard by the viral moment's reach, but felt it was "amazing" that the clip was "opening a conversation" and inviting more women to talk about their experiences. "The reaction has been wild," she related on *The Ryan Tubridy Show*. "It's definitely not something that I had expected, and I didn't necessarily set out to sort of make a splash. But I do think there's something really telling about the society that we're in right now, and how open women want to be with the men in their lives. So many men and women that I know from all over the world have gotten in touch with me about this one comment." She also urged that people watch the clip in its entire context, to see that the male stars weren't "debunking" her assertion—the point was that they would have missed it otherwise.

She spoke up because she is accustomed to doing so, and the issue at hand was one she has refused to shy away from. "It felt very similar to when I am at a dinner with a bunch of my friends, and I will always make the point that, well, this is actually an experience that we go through every single day, one hundred percent."

In fact, Saoirse discussed the moment with her friend Paul Mescal in the immediate aftermath, concerned about how it would play out and be perceived when the episode aired. "I came away from filming it; Paul and I went for a drink afterwards, and I was so in my head about it," she said on the podcast *Table Manners with Jessie Ware*. "Maybe two days later, once it had aired—I was anxious about it airing—then my best mate said, 'Everyone's contacting me about the phone comment.' I'm very grateful for one comment that I've made to have started a conversation that absolutely needs to be had." While Saoirse didn't anticipate the global dialogue that resulted, she declared that she felt "incredibly refreshed and proud."

This extraordinary sequence of events—Saoirse speaking up, finding just the right words, her graciousness in wanting to redirect any backlash from the other guests, her thoughtfulness in furthering the discussion and bravely standing by her words for social good—all of this encapsulates who Saoirse Ronan is in a nutshell. Her public persona is an electrifying mix of contradictions. She is a bold, whip-smart thinker unafraid to give voice to the causes she cares deeply

Saoirse in *Atonement*, 2007.

Following: Saoirse poses during the British Academy Scotland Awards, November 2022.

"I'm very **grateful** for one **comment** that I've made to have started a **conversation** that **absolutely** needs to be had."

about, while also caring deeply about the impact of her words and worrying about their reception. She is known for her down-to-earth mentality, widely reputed to be warm, funny, grounded, and plugged in to the zeitgeist—the sort of person internet denizens call "mother." Yet at the same time, despite these long-standing perceptions of her, she has carefully guarded her privacy when the camera stops rolling. Going viral as herself—instead of a meme derived from one of her famous characters, or because she wore an eye-catching dress to an awards ceremony—was an entirely new experience.

Though Saoirse has been on the big screen for almost two decades, ever since she burst onto the scene and earned her first Academy Award nomination at age thirteen playing young Briony in *Atonement*, she has maintained a boundary between her public and private lives. Despite twenty years in Hollywood, an armload of awards and nominations, and dozens of movie productions, she's the sort of person who is humble about her status and seems surprised to be recognized as a celebrity. "I still get completely shocked that anyone knows who I am," she told *Vogue* in 2018. "I'm not famous . . . I just genuinely don't think I am. Selena Gomez is famous."

But Saoirse *is* famous and regularly included in lists that tout the best actors of the century. In the years prior to that *Vogue* statement, she had already secured three Academy Award nominations, to which she would go on to add another for the lead role of Jo March in *Little Women*. That's four nominations for Hollywood's top prize, all before the age of thirty.

Saoirse wasn't displaying false humility when she claimed she could fly under the radar, however. While cinephiles adore Saoirse and are quick to praise her versatile and daring acting roles, she doesn't have the instant recognition or reputation attached to other big stars who live their private lives in the open. She has never shied away from publicity when it comes to her work—gracing magazine covers, delighting the viewing audience with lively interviews, making a splash with her impeccable fashion on the red carpet, or speaking out about politics in the countries where she is a citizen (Ireland and the US). But she has largely eschewed becoming the tabloid fodder. When not on set, she lives by all accounts a low-key lifestyle with her husband, Scottish actor Jack Lowden, a relationship developed so far from paparazzi lenses that their engagement was only discovered by sharp-eyed observers of Lowden's Instagram. (Intrepid fans correctly deciphered that an unidentified hand wearing a ring was Saoirse's.)

It's impossible to imagine Saoirse Ronan courting attention, as some celebrities do, by inviting the press in, arranging a newly decorated mansion, or for curating wedding pictures to be splashed across the pages of glossy magazines. Quite consciously and deliberately, Saoirse keeps herself to herself, a practice that started in

Saoirse at the Annual Palm Springs International Film Festival Awards Gala, January 2018.

the early days of her career. *Vogue* noted that "as a child star, [she] was not expected to divulge details about her private life, because children are not generally thought to have private lives." When she became an accomplished teenage actress, and then a celebrated leading lady, Saoirse continued the patterns learned in childhood.

"I think people know not to ask me certain things," she affirmed to *Vogue*. "They're not going to know who I'm going out with or where I live. They're not going to know much about my family." A single-minded focus on her craft has always been with her. "When I'm working, I can't really do anything else. I can't go out, I can't meet up with anyone, I don't read anything. Someone said to me, 'You're monogamous when it comes to your work,' and it's so true. You can only commit to one thing at a time." As a result, Saoirse is a unique and fascinating force in Hollywood: an unquestioned virtuoso in her field, a dazzling success hailed as a generational talent, and yet still, at home and with her loved ones, a regular person who is surprised to be pointed out on the street.

"When I'm working, I can't really do anything else. I can't go out, I can't meet up with anyone, I don't read anything. Someone said to me, 'You're monogamous when it comes to your work,' and it's so true."

For many around the world who caught the viral *Graham Norton Show* clip as it blew up on TikTok or was replayed on the morning news, it may have been the first time they glimpsed Saoirse in action beyond her acclaimed body of cinematic and theatrical work. It's remarkable to see a celebrity renowned for being "real"—someone willing to advocate for social justice without mincing words, someone unwilling to stay silent—who is also somewhat of a cipher, absent from social media and other avenues that pry into personal space.

Saoirse Ronan is ever the consummate actor: game, sparkling, and outspoken when the cameras are trained on her. Outside of the lights, she draws a line around her life, inspired by the protective barriers her parents took care to maintain as she came of age under Hollywood's notoriously unforgiving glare. In order to trace her astonishing and inspiring rise to prominence, and to understand how she came to be on a late-night talk show and got the whole world talking with just a few words, it's essential to go back to the beginning. Like all good stories, this one involves a perilous journey, and the lasting impact of friends met along the way.

From the Bronx to Ireland to Hollywood

chapter 1

"From the day she was young, she was always a very confident little child—and I knew she'd make a good actor."

—Paul Ronan to *RSVP Live*

Saoirse Úna Ronan was born on April 12, 1994, in New York City. Fittingly, that makes her an Aries—the Zodiac sign under which people are said to be bold, passionate, and courageous, marked by confidence and an eagerness to undertake new projects. Aries are fun and lively, make loyal friends, and have a determined, ambitious streak—if you're a fan of astrology, it's not a huge leap to imagine that Saoirse's path was influenced by her stars.

She has been fielding questions about what *Vogue* called her "famously difficult" name for as long as she's been in the public

---

Saoirse Ronan in *I Could Never Be Your Woman*, 2007.

sphere, approaching the inquiry with good humor. "'Seer-sha' is how Irish people pronounce my first name," she explained, "but I would pronounce it 'Sir-sha,' like 'inertia.' It's Irish for 'freedom.' I recently found out that my middle name, Úna, means 'unity' in Ireland. And I think my last name means 'seal.' So I'm a free, unified seal."

Saoirse's name is a frequent talking point in interviews and profiles about her, so much so that she has these amusing responses tucked into her back pocket, ready to be deployed. It reached a peak when she hosted *Saturday Night Live* in 2017. Her opening monologue took the form of a comedic song about teaching people how to pronounce her name. "Yes, I am very Irish, and I have an extremely Irish name, some would say *too* Irish," she says dryly. "But I've got a little problem. It's spelled wrong. It's a full typo . . . You can see why people have a hard time. If it were a *Wheel of Fortune* puzzle, you couldn't afford it. Too many vowels!"

Saoirse's parents, Paul and Monica, were part of a wave of young Irish people who sought opportunities abroad in the 1980s and '90s, when the Irish economy was faltering. "Mom and [dad] just came over to work—a lot of that generation chose work over college because it was kind of the more realistic route at the time," Saoirse told *New York Magazine*. Many followed the pathways carved out by Irish immigrants in the decades and the century before, landing in communities that still had a strong Irish center and could offer some support upon arrival. For Paul and Monica, who were both from Dublin, that meant Woodlawn in New York City. Situated at the northern edge of the Bronx, Woodlawn is part of an area dubbed "Little Ireland." Irish pubs and cultural centers dot the avenues, while Irish flags hang in shop windows. It has been a bustling center of Irish activity and a place for newly arrived immigrants to find a foothold since the late 1800s.

What's in a Name?

Saoirse always approaches the name question, and the subsequent lessons she has to teach, with her keen wit and customary graciousness. But it would be nice if TV hosts and celebrity profilers could move on—or at least explore the *why* behind the name instead of the *how-to-say-it*. Her name's pronunciation has been explained over and over again, yet rarely do discussions touch upon its true significance, which is a richer vein to mine. Saoirse, as she mentioned, means "freedom" in Irish Gaelic, and it began reviving in popularity as a name in the 1920s as a symbol of the Irish fight for independence from Britain. It is both a constant reference to freedom and a declaration of it. In 1922, the Irish War of Independence resulted in the establishment of "Saorstát Éireann," or the Irish Free State.

Saoirse Úna's name in full—freedom, unity—reflects the turbulence of Ireland's history and celebrates its liberation. "In historical accounts, the name Saoirse emerges as a symbol of resistance against oppressive forces," *Ancestry* writes. "In the early twentieth century, Saoirse served as a rallying cry for freedom . . . This name echoed the unwavering spirit of the Irish people, who yearned to reclaim their autonomy and preserve their culture against all odds." It's an important name, steeped in Irish pride and history, given to a baby girl born in America to Irish parents.

Saoirse Ronan takes part in a photocall at the Burlington Hotel in Dublin, May 2012.

Saoirse for the Coca-Cola Cinemagic International Film and Television Festival for Young People, Dublin, Ireland, May 2011.

SAOIRSE FROM THE BLOCK

Saoirse only lived with her parents in the Bronx until age three, when the family made the move back to Ireland. As such, she has a unique recollection of her birthplace. "I have these sort of nonspecific memories," she told *The Providence Journal.* "They are really more sensorial, emotional memories, but they couldn't have happened anywhere else." This New Yorker origin story would come back into play, and it would lead to significant decisions in Saoirse's career, like starring as a young Irish immigrant who makes a parallel journey to that of her parents in her movie *Brooklyn* and her eventual Broadway debut. "I remember them happening in New York," she said of her earliest recollections, "and I think, because of that, when I eventually started visiting New York in my teens, the connection that I had to the city was just so powerful, so strong. It really made me feel that this was the city I wanted to end up living in."

While living in New York, Saoirse's parents encountered the sorts of struggles that can often emerge in the immigrant experience. Theirs were specific to being undocumented in America, a topic that Saoirse always addresses with frankness. "They lived in a terrible little apartment in the Bronx and because they were illegals, they were really badly treated and did some awful jobs," she shared with *Radio Times.* Of their financial situation during these years, she explained, "We weren't poor, but we didn't have money."

Over the decades, in many interviews, Saoirse has spoken about the difficult choices and conditions that her parents faced as undocumented immigrants—one of the rare cases where Saoirse reveals personal details and draws back the curtain on her private life. As with her viral moment on *Norton,* she is invested in directing greater awareness and sympathy to experiences that can be overlooked and are too often politicized, to the detriment of erasing the reality that people endure. "They had nothing, and they were illegal for a few years so they couldn't leave because they wouldn't be allowed back in," she told *The Daily Telegraph.* Her mother wanted to make sure that Saoirse would

"She was adamant that she was going to have me there [in America] so I wouldn't ever have to go through the tough time that they had in order to get their visas."

not face the same kind of conflict. "She was adamant that she was going to have me there [in America] so I wouldn't ever have to go through the tough time that they had in order to get their visas." Monica took jobs as a nanny and cleaner, while Paul worked in construction and later as a bartender. It was Paul's bartending gig that would have an unexpectedly seismic impact on the young family. "A lot of Irish actors would go in [to the bar] and they got to know him," Saoirse related, "and one of them eventually asked him to audition for a play."

The man, Chris O'Neill, who asked Paul to audition for a play, changed the course of the Ronans' trajectory and laid the groundwork for Saoirse to emerge as an international superstar a decade later. "If it wasn't for Chris, neither of us would be acting today," Saoirse told *Radio Times*. In 1991, O'Neill cofounded The Bronx Irish Theatre Company, with the mission to stage productions steeped in authentic Irish stories and experiences. He was a regular at the downtown Manhattan bar, O'Hanlon's, where Paul worked, and he spotted potential in the affable bartender. He gave Paul free theater tickets and encouraged his love

Saoirse in *The Lovely Bones*, 2009.

for the stage. Then he was insistent that Paul himself audition. "I didn't know what an audition was; I didn't know what to do. And I don't know if it was because I had a bit of a hard neck and I was a bit cocky, I said 'ah, I'll give it a go!'" Paul recalled to *RSVP Live*.

After Paul was cast in O'Neill's production of the play *Da* by Hugh Leonard, he caught the acting bug and never looked back. Only later did he realize how much O'Neill had helped him on his way: "What I didn't know until afterwards was that I was the only one auditioning. He didn't want anyone else." O'Neill took Paul under his wing, casting him in many shows that led to further opportunities and the dedicated life of a working actor. "To this day, I've never taken any classes or anything—I've always learned on the job," Paul said. This would turn out to be the exact model of dramatic training that Saoirse undertook—though she did not follow in her father's footsteps per se. She was carried along with him, quite literally. Paul often took his young daughter to play rehearsals, and in later years, to TV and film sets. He starred on Irish television and in major Hollywood productions like *The Devil's Own, Veronica Guerin,* and *The Boxer.*

"Paul would show up with his little girl, Saoirse, and plop her down beside me while he rehearsed," actor and writer Colin Broderick wrote in his memoir of their time doing plays with Chris O'Neill. Acting, and being surrounded by actors, was a sort of daycare for Saoirse—a given state for her to be in, and foundational to her life. Is it any surprise that she's such a natural on-screen? "He just learned on the job," Saoirse said of her father's training, echoing his own words. Her father's learn-by-doing approach would perfectly mirror how Saoirse came to be an actor. "I think it was the best way for both of us—it shaped how we work."

FIRST STEPS ON-SCREEN

Paul Ronan foresaw his daughter's future at an early age. "From the day she was young, she was always a very confident little child—and I knew she'd make a good actor," he told *RSVP Live*. His encouragement and advocacy were central to Saoirse's development in what would become

Saoirse in *The Lovely Bones*, 2009.

the family business, and he was over the moon to witness Saoirse's burgeoning potential. "I loved it so much that I encouraged her, and I put her in a short film when she was five years of age." By this time, the Ronans had returned to Ireland and were living in County Carlow, a relatively rural area in the country's southeast. Paul had an agent and was working steadily enough to use his connections to broaden Saoirse's opportunities.

"After the short film, I introduced her to my agent and we started doing auditions," he went on. Saoirse's first on-screen roles saw her guest-starring for episodic stints on two Irish TV productions—the medical drama *The Clinic* and the crime thriller *Proof*. Saoirse was nine and ten, respectively, when she was broadcast on the Irish airways. She had a rather dramatic reaction to her first acting job, a sign of how deeply she was invested in her calling from the start. "I went into this melancholic state for a few weeks," she told *Vogue* of the time when her work on *The Clinic* was concluded. "I remember sitting on the bed with Mam next to me, and I was like: 'I'm never going to have that experience again. That exact crew will never work together again. Never.'" Such depth of emotion is fitting for such a natural-born actor, and though she didn't know it yet, Saoirse would be stepping onto a road set to take her through this loop over and over again.

Her skill and promise when performing had already been established in a *somewhat* smaller venue: for school plays in the little village of Ardattin, County Carlow (population: 34), where she attended primary school. "I remember her very first role was as a tree," teacher Kathleen Bolger told *The Irish Independent* of five-year-old Saoirse's "stage debut." "She was great. She loved it." *The Irish Independent* documented the further course of Saoirse taking the stage at school: "In Senior Infants she played a rat in *The Pied Piper of Hamlin,* and Kathleen recalls she was 'a very good rat!', adding that Saoirse progressed to playing the Pied Piper himself the following year." Even as a young student, Saoirse's career mapped a trajectory that would prove prophetic: smaller roles demonstrated what enormous talent she possessed, causing her to leap ahead and land squarely in the spotlight.

After Saoirse's roles on Irish television, her career reached a turning point. "Her third job was with Michelle Pfeiffer in *I Could Never Be Your Woman,* and from there, that was it," Paul Ronan told *RSVP Live.* The

Saoirse and Michelle Pfeiffer in *I Could Never Be Your Woman,* 2007.

2007 romantic comedy film, written and directed by *Clueless*'s Amy Heckerling, starred Michelle Pfeiffer and Paul Rudd, with eleven-year-old Saoirse playing Pfeiffer's thirteen-year-old daughter, Izzie. While audiences and critics didn't flock to the movie with a *Clueless*-like fervor, Saoirse's performance received its first glowing reviews.

> "I remember her very first role was as a tree . . . She was great. She loved it."
>
> —Saoirse's teacher, Kathleen Bolger.

Soon the move was made to homeschool Saoirse, as she told *Vogue*, "because I was on set so much." She also attributed the decision to leave traditional school to growing pains with her newfound celebrity. She explained to *The Guardian*, "The reason was teachers giving me a hard time. Teachers and students . . . Some of the students were, you know, mean. But I only stayed a while. It wasn't really working out. You know, the school is a good school and the people who go there are good people. But when your schoolmates recognize you before they've met you, and the teachers do, too, it can make things very awkward and difficult. It's a shame." At the time, Saoirse's star was rising and would go supernova with *Atonement*, which brought her global acclaim and her first Academy Award nomination at the age of thirteen. Her parents were there every step of the way, traveling with Saoirse, staying with her, coordinating her press, and supervising her on set in a bid to keep the burgeoning star protected.

In interviews and appearances, Saoirse credits her parents for keeping her grounded and safe. Too often, the pitfalls of fast fame, money, and relentless attention can have a devastating effect on children and young adults in show business. The Ronans did everything they could to ensure that kind of fate would not befall Saoirse. She is always quick to highlight the close relationship she has with her mother, Monica, and point out how integral Monica's influence was on safeguarding her during her most vulnerable years.

“I don’t know what would have happened if she [her mother] hadn’t been around,” Saoirse told *Harper’s Bazaar UK* in 2019. Referencing the #MeToo movement and the abuses of power in Hollywood that were being revealed, she said, “I’m sure I would have been exposed to that quite a bit, but she just protected me from all that.” While Saoirse wasn’t kept swaddled from the realities of her industry, her mother’s active intervention ensured that she was not directly subjected to it. “I wasn’t unaware that there were people in the industry who abused their power, or who were seedy or untrustworthy,” she explained. “But because of her I was never a victim and I’m very, very thankful.” She concluded, “I hadn’t been wrapped in cotton wool, but I had been protected.”

In another interview, Saoirse related that she’d discussed the importance of her mother’s early intervention with another actor who could understand—nearly exactly—the strange movie-set environment in which she grew up. “I was talking to someone who started out as a child actor, last night, and went on to do incredible things,” she told *The Cut*, “and we were both saying it was a huge, huge influence to have our mothers with us when we were young, and mothers who came from more of an ethical standpoint than a business one. To have someone with you from ten to nineteen when you’re on a set, who has perspective and is only there to look out for you, it really means that you have a more realistic way of looking at this entire world. [It was] Jodie Foster.”

Her parents’ sensible approach also produced a daughter who wanted to experience “real life,” despite rocketing to the heights of fame in her youth. “I never wanted to just be, you know, a child actor who grew up in this unrealistic world where, okay, you’re working hard, but everything’s done for you,” she related to *Time Out*. “I think it was Emma Thompson who said to me years ago that if you’re going to portray normal people, you need to have a normal life.”

"I don't know what would have happened if she [her mother] hadn't been around."

Greatest Champion: Mam

Saoirse has remained exceptionally close to her mother, Monica. A 2015 profile from *The Gentlewoman* called the two "soulmates," drawing from Saoirse's own description. Writer Sophie Elmhirst traveled to Howth, a small town outside Dublin where Saoirse was visiting her mother. "To understand Saoirse, you have to meet her mother," Elmhirst wrote. "Partly because her daughter describes Monica as her 'soulmate,' but also because when you meet her, you realize why Saoirse—a child star and thus almost inevitably a human catastrophe—turned out OK. They don't look much alike—Monica is short, wiry, and dark—but they finish each other's sentences and make each other howl with laughter."

Saoirse told Elmhirst that Monica was "the perfect movie mam," because "she wasn't one of those crazy mothers who was living vicariously through me, or so crazy protective that she wouldn't let anyone do anything. But she protected me and kept me away from all the grown-up stuff that can kind of ruin you a bit when you're a kid."

What was Monica's approach to parenting a burgeoning star? "Teaching them respect when they're on set," Monica explained. "They're not queen bee. There are a lot of people running around after you, and when you're a small child you can easily get used to it. You have to teach them."

"It doesn't even feel like it's enough to say that we're close," Saoirse said, at a loss for how to describe the unique relationship with her mother. "We're just part of each other, y'know?"

Saoirse and her mother at the ISPCC Luncheon, September 2013.

Eilis Lacey in *Brooklyn*

Starring in the 2015 movie *Brooklyn* was a watershed moment in Saoirse's career. Not only did the role earn her a second Academy Award nomination at age twenty-one—this time for Best Actress—but she was embodying a character close to her heart and to both of the countries she has called home. In director John Crowley's adaptation of Colm Tóibín's acclaimed novel, Saoirse plays Eilis Lacey, a young woman who immigrates from Ireland to New York City in the 1950s.

Eilis leaves her small town in Ireland due to a lack of opportunities there but struggles to adjust to life in the bustling metropolis. Slowly she finds her way and begins to build a promising future—making friends, excelling at studies, and falling in love with the sweet, charming Tony (Emory Cohen), an Italian-American plumber. Just when it seems that Eilis's life has taken root in America and is set to bloom, tragedy brings her back to Ireland. She rediscovers the comforts of home and finds herself tempted by the prospects of another romance, courted by well-to-do, erudite Jim (Domhnall Gleeson). Eilis must decide where she truly belongs.

"It was the first time in my career where my personal life and my character's life paralleled in every way," she told *The Providence Journal*. "Certainly, the experience of leaving home was something that I had gone through myself. And the relationship with America, with New York, was something that I could really appreciate." Later she came to understand how much Eilis's immigrant experience had mirrored her parents' own journey. "I only realized in retrospect that it is essentially their story," she related in an interview with the *Daily Telegraph*. When she took her mother to the film's premiere at Sundance, "For me, she was the most important critic, because I wanted her to feel like it had authentically portrayed her struggle."

Chapter 2

Starting Small and Young

"Then along came Saoirse Ronan, and that piece of casting allowed the film to be what it became . . . we were very lucky."

—Director Joe Wright on *Atonement*

Saoirse had begun to establish a reputation as a talented child actor in Irish TV dramas and small-scale Hollywood films, but few could have predicted what the next few years would bring. She was soon to experience a career propulsion into the stratosphere, going "from zero to sixty in no time at all," as *USA Today* put it. Just prior to this meteoric rise, however, there was a longed-for part that she lost out on—the role of Luna Lovegood in *Harry Potter and the Order of the Phoenix.*

Warner Bros. Studios cast a wide net to find their Luna. The fan-favorite character is a brave and sweetly eccentric Irish student at the Hogwarts School of Witchcraft & Wizardry who befriends Harry Potter and joins his adventures. In January of 2006, when the studio held an

---

Previous: Saoirse as Eilis Lacey in *Brooklyn*, 2015.

Saoirse attends the *Atonement* premiere in London, September 2007.

open audition for the coveted part, more than fifteen thousand hopeful Lunas answered the call. Saoirse and many of her fellow young Irish actors were among those eager to join the *Harry Potter* franchise. Years later she recalled on *Jimmy Kimmel Live!*, "Because it was the Irish character, so they got everyone Irish in, like, 'Half Ireland, come and audition.'"

Saoirse was only twelve when she auditioned to play Luna. She was ultimately too young for the role, which went to fourteen-year-old—the age Luna is meant to be in the movie—Evanna Lynch. While it's intriguing to imagine an alternate universe where Saoirse Ronan got to attend Hogwarts, what happened next was even more magical. In 2007, the year that *Harry Potter and the Order of the Phoenix* hit the screens, Saoirse would be nominated for an Oscar for her performance in *Atonement*, and her life would never be the same.

AN UNCONVENTIONAL CASTING

Saoirse also auditioned for *Atonement* when she was twelve—and the ages of the actor and the character were in perfect alignment. She was going up for the pivotal role of Briony Tallis, who is thirteen—a sheltered, naive thirteen at that—in the first part of the film.

In Ian McEwan's bestselling novel *Atonement*, young Briony is a privileged member of the English landed gentry, living at her family's sprawling country estate in 1935. A creative and stubborn child with a penchant for writing and making up stories, Briony has been raised in a world of luxury, rigid class divides, and sheltered innocence that begets ignorance.

It is Briony's status and the unfounded accusation she makes that sets the plot into explosive motion. The movie adaptation follows Briony through three stages of her life: a seemingly idyllic youth transformed by one fateful night and one unforgivable lie; as a young woman serving as a trauma nurse in wartime; and as an elderly author reflecting back on the ruinous consequences of her childhood mistake.

Ireland forever

Though Saoirse's fast-moving career at an early age meant that she would soon be on film sets all over the world, Ireland has remained a constant source of passion and pride. "Ronan loves her country. Not in a generically patriotic, home-loving way, but with the burn of history at her back," noted a 2015 profile in *The Gentlewoman*. "She admires figures such as James Connolly and Patrick Pearse for their struggle against English rule; she wants to play Mary, Queen of Scots . . . because she can relate to the politics, to the history of Scotland and its struggle."

This love of country would also lead to participating in movies that had a seismic impact on Saoirse's life and career, like *Brooklyn*. *The Gentlewoman* said that Saoirse was "visibly moved" in discussing her role in that production "because it's a genuine, unclichéd representation of Ireland and was adapted from an Irish book, made by an Irish director, and performed by an Irish cast." They write that "Ireland is her home, but it's also her passion." Saoirse has maintained that passion, working as an advocate for Irish charities and causes, and actively campaigning for its progressive movements. She also credits her background for her work ethic and for keeping her centered. She told *The Independent* in 2019 that the "brilliant" circle of Irish stars and creatives are fiercely supportive of each other, "because we come from a small place and we know how big a thing it is to go out there."

Saoirse in *Brooklyn*, 2015.

The choice of who would play young Briony was one of director Joe Wright's most crucial decisions, and he decided to take a huge gamble on a relatively unknown child actor who at first glance did not fit the bill for the character one bit. "Briony was supposed to be this brown-haired, brown-eyed, middle-class English girl—she was supposed to look like she was related to Keira [Knightley, who plays Briony's sister Cecilia]," Saoirse said in a 2016 interview with *Time*.

The Irish Mirror reported on Wright's recollections of casting Saoirse—and his astonishment at finding out that her background did not resemble Briony Tallis's at all. "We met many, many kids for that role. Then we were sent this tape of this little girl speaking in this perfect 1920s English accent," Wright said. "Immediately, she had this kind of intensity, dynamism, and willfulness." When Saoirse came in person to audition for the role, the director was surprised at how skillful an act she had put on from the start. "When we got her to come over to London to meet and read with us, I was shocked to discover this little Irish kid who spoke with a thick Irish accent. I thought maybe there'd been a mistake. And then I sat down to read with her, and as soon as she started reading, I realized she was an extraordinary talent."

In a 2018 profile with *The Independent,* on his decade-plus filmmaking career, Wright explained that discovering Saoirse was the final piece that enabled the film to come together and match the vision he had internally. "I had a secret about it," he said of *Atonement*. "I could see the film so clearly in my head. It was so much about form as much as content, and the form reflected the content so perfectly. I was so excited about it. I kind of muddled through *Pride and Prejudice* but with *Atonement,* I knew what I was doing. That makes it sound like I had no doubt—I had doubts; I didn't know whether it would work. But I knew exactly what I wanted to try to do." That sense of certainty finally came once Saoirse was found. "Then along came Saoirse Ronan," Wright went on, "and that piece of casting allowed the film to be what it became . . . we were very lucky."

"I thought maybe there'd been a mistake. And then I sat down to read with her, and as soon as she started reading, I realized she was an extraordinary talent."

—Director Joe Wright on Saoirse, 2018

Saoirse and James McAvoy in *Atonement*, 2007.

Saoirse also uses the word "luck" in relation to *Atonement,* but she applies it to how she got the opportunity to be seen and recognized by Wright in the first place. "This dialect coach suggested me, even though I was completely wrong for it," she explained in a *Time* interview, musing: "It's funny, because you can work as hard as possible, but if you don't have a bit of luck and someone who puts your name forward, you may not get anywhere."

Some actors would look back and frame their breakthrough audition as being seen as an irresistible force of nature or an undeniable talent that was duly recognized. And, certainly, Joe Wright says that he saw this in Saoirse. But Saoirse herself is more circumspect. In a move that is a recurring theme throughout her interviews and public appearances over the years, she points to the contributions of other people in helping to pave her way forward—here, the dialect coach whom she worked with on *I Can Never Be Your Woman* and who paved the way to *Atonement.* She often highlights the impact of a movie's crew or costume designer or assistant director—and she credits "luck," not as a mystical sort of blessing, but as something that other people have helped anoint her with.

It's clear from Wright's remarks, however, that he felt the luck was on *his* side in encountering Saoirse. It's a remarkable thing for a director to declare the casting of a twelve-year-old as the turning point in a movie—one who would go on to be nominated for dozens of awards and win several, including a Golden Globe and an Oscar. Especially since the cast already had Keira Knightley, James McAvoy, Benedict Cumberbatch, Alfie Allen, Brenda Blethyn, and Juno Temple. All were either acting luminaries at the outset or would see *Atonement* vault them into distinguished careers. A child star who only appears in the movie's first chapter would often be a footnote in a production like this.

But what happened with Saoirse's Briony was a perfect storm of an unforgettable character matched with an unforgettable performance. Ask most people today what they remember about *Atonement* and they'll list three things: Keira Knightley's dazzling green flapper dress, iconic enough to have its own dedicated Wikipedia page; the library love scene between Knightley and McAvoy's characters, which showcased their molten chemistry; and Saoirse Ronan as the complicated, flawed, bright, misguided, and much-maligned young Briony Tallis.

Keira Knightley and Saoirse in *Atonement*, 2007.

While Saoirse continued to be safeguarded by her parents' advocacy for years to come, the degree of relative obscurity she experienced while filming *Atonement* would never quite be accessible again. It would be the movie that changed everything for her. The film was a critical and box-office hit, with glowing reviews to match. On the review aggregation site Metacritic, it has a score of 85 from reviewers in 2007, indicating "universal acclaim." On Rotten Tomatoes, which also factors in reviews from the years since release, it holds "fresh" at 83 percent positive. *Atonement* earned $129 million on a budget of $30 million, further establishing Joe Wright's filmmaking prowess and burnishing the star power of leads Knightley and McAvoy. Many critics named it on their lists of Top 10 films of the year, including Roger Ebert, the *Los Angeles Times, The New York Times, Rolling Stone,* and *The Wall Street Journal*. It received seven nominations for the 65th Golden Globe Awards, more than any other movie nominated that year, and won the night's biggest prize: Best Motion Picture—Drama. Saoirse, James McAvoy, and Keira Knightley were all nominated for Golden Globes for their acting, though only one of them—Saoirse—would carry that nomination over to the Academy Awards.

A SPARK IGNITES

It's not feasible to talk about *Atonement*'s success and Saoirse's subsequent rise as separate phenomena. They are inextricably bound. As entertainment site Collider wrote, "Ronan was the person who truly stole everyone's fascination in *Atonement*."

Christopher Orr, writing for *The Atlantic*, said that "Ronan's younger version is a marvel, elegantly capturing the narcissism and self-doubt that adhere to precocity," while David Ansen of *Newsweek* called her "a captivating presence." Ty Burr from *The Boston Globe* went with "a marvel" and Lou Lumenick of *The New York Post* deemed her "astounding."

In an article for Collider in 2024, Jacob Slankard revisited the *Atonement* era with a headline that summarized all of this neatly: "Saoirse Ronan's Performance in *Atonement* Was So Good, It Made Us Hate a Child." Slankard wrote, "Of the many prominent actresses we currently have, few have the ability to overpower a character's flaws with their natural intrigue, like Saoirse Ronan. She's had a career defined by a hiding-in-plain-sight quality, creating a gap between her exterior display and her interior truth that makes us want to lean forward and decipher what she's really thinking."

Hollywood was convinced from the get-go, with Saoirse's Oscar nomination for Best Supporting Actress in *Atonement*. This anointed Saoirse as not only someone to watch, but someone positioned for greatness. At thirteen years old, she became the seventh-youngest actor ever nominated in her category.

She attended the Oscars ceremony in 2008 with her parents, flying over from New Zealand, where she was filming Peter Jackson's *The Lovely Bones*. Saoirse wore a dress by Alberta Ferretti in a bright, vibrant green embellished with jewels and delicate lace embroidery.

As for her first Oscars, the experience appears to have been overwhelming. In her signature grounded fashion, Saoirse often shares relatable fish-out-of-water stories and anecdotes from others when asked to recount how she felt as a first-time nominee. In an

"Honestly, the thing that excited me the most about it was that I had watched the Oscars on the telly every year that it was on since I was very, very young, so the fact that I was getting to go and be a part of it . . . I was so excited about that more than anything."

interview at the Santa Barbara International Film Festival, Saoirse said, "Honestly, the thing that excited me the most about it was that I had watched the Oscars on the telly every year that it was on since I was very, very young, so the fact that I was getting to go and be a part of it . . . I was so excited about that more than anything." She said that Peter Jackson gave her some advice before she left for the show, "because he's obviously won like fifty-five Oscars and is very experienced when it comes to the Academy." Jackson's advice, according to Saoirse, was that "it's gonna go by so quickly, so you

(left to right) James McAvoy, Saoirse Ronan, Vanessa Redgrave, Joe Wright, and Keira Knightley arrive for the screening of *Atonement*, 2007.

just need to take a second to soak it all up and really sort of immerse yourself in it. So that's what I did. It was brilliant. It was great."

Saoirse lost out on the Best Supporting Actress statuette, which went to Tilda Swinton for *Michael Clayton*, but to receive a nomination at such a young age was a significant acknowledgment from both the power brokers and her peers in Hollywood. Such an early boost does not, however, guarantee a lifetime of success or immediate promotion into Hollywood's elite ranks.

Instead of chasing the biggest paychecks or parts in the trendiest films of the moment, Saoirse took on an eclectic range of roles in a run of wildly different movies, ensuring that she was never boxed in to play a certain kind of character. She worked tirelessly, adding to her already considerable skillset with new accents and rigorous physical training, and performing against special effects backdrops.

Saoirse would come to be recognized as *the* go-to actor for the coming-of-age narrative, receiving some of the best reviews of her career and a bevy of award nominations for her lead roles in *Brooklyn, Lady Bird,* and *Little Women*. In her *actual* coming-of-age period, however, she was rarely seen performing as a traditional teenager. As she viewed clips from some of her most famous movies for a *Vanity Fair* video feature in 2024, Saoirse mused, "The experience of watching something when you're an adult is completely different, because the movies that I made when I was growing up, they were mature. They were not children's films at all." She could tally the number of PG-rated or young adult films she made as a child on one hand. "I think I made one, two kids' movies, and the rest were incredibly mature."

The experience of taking part in films with more adult themes didn't mean that Saoirse was made to engage with the full reality of them. Her parents, directors, and costars worked diligently to keep her shielded. In fact, this unique on-set education and training—tailored to her youth—ended up having a profound impact on the way that she still approaches acting.

Saoirse and director Peter Jackson on the set of *The Lovely Bones*, 2009.

THE NEXT BIG ROLE

One of the movies after *Atonement* where a shielded approach proved to be vital was *The Lovely Bones*, filmed when Saoirse was fourteen. "Even with something like *The Lovely Bones*," she told *Vanity Fair*, "I think the sort of gravity of that really didn't hit me at the time. And I actually watched a sequence from it recently and I found it incredibly disturbing, and I didn't want to watch it again." It's testament to the care director Peter Jackson took with Saoirse on the set, as well as her parents' watchful eye, that the weight of the movie's subject matter didn't appear to impact her at fourteen.

Adapted from the 2002 best-selling novel by Alice Sebold, *The Lovely Bones* follows a girl named Susie Salmon living in small-town Pennsylvania in 1973. Susie is the same age as Saoirse while filming when she is assaulted and murdered by her neighbor. Susie is then trapped in an "in-between," dead but not moving on. She serves as the movie's narrator, observing her family and friends in the aftermath

"When she's performing—when she's in the moment—there's no sense that she's acting."

—Peter Jackson on Saoirse, 2009

of her disappearance as well as watching her killer, over the span of many years.

In a 2009 article on Saoirse and *The Lovely Bones*, the *LA Times* reported that Saoirse and her parents were initially hesitant to accept the role because of the heavy themes, "[b]ut after meeting with Jackson, their hesitation eased." Saoirse elaborated in a 2010 *Globe and Mail* piece: "From the off, Pete didn't want to make a movie where you see a child being sexually assaulted and murdered. It's happened a lot in movies where it completely overwhelms the story, and the story is so much more than that. That was the deal-maker for me."

"When she's performing—when she's in the moment—there's no sense that she's acting," Jackson told the *LA Times* of Saoirse. "It just feels completely authentic. I can see her being one of the premium actresses of her generation. It's impossible to predict things, but she's so versatile. I could easily see her having a career as esteemed as Cate Blanchett or Kate Winslet." When it came to Saoirse's eventual career trajectory, it would appear that Peter Jackson had the gift of prophecy. Soon enough Saoirse would be acting alongside Blanchett in the action/thriller *Hanna* and, in later years, play Winslet's love interest in *Ammonite*. In addition to Blanchett and Winslet, soon comparisons with a young Meryl Streep were added to the mix.

Saoirse's performance in *The Lovely Bones* received widespread praise, although the movie itself received mixed reviews upon release. With its difficult subject matter and many scenes filled in postproduction with elaborate special effects that depict Susie's supernatural purgatory, the film divided critics. The movie emerged at a time when computer-generated imagery (CGI) was gaining prominence but was not always so seamlessly applied by directors or accepted by viewers. *The Globe and Mail* said that "at times [Jackson's] fantastical heaven can overwhelm what's happening down on earth," but noted that "even though she had to do much of her acting alone, in front of a blue screen," Saoirse "expertly communicates both Susie's human panic and her post-mortem wafting."

With only a 31 percent rating on Rotten Tomatoes, *The Lovely Bones* is not beloved by a majority of cinephiles. But it would firmly establish a theme that endures for Saoirse since her film debut and in every film thereafter: even when critics take issue with a production she appears in, her performance is held up as a standout. Giving *The Lovely Bones* one and a half stars and a scathing review in *The Chicago Sun-Times,* legendary film critic Roger Ebert still wrote that Saoirse was "a very good young actress, who cannot be faulted here."

Saoirse also received equally winning reviews from her costars, with Stanley Tucci telling the *LA Times,* "She handles herself as well as any seasoned actor. I wouldn't even be able to finish a sentence at her age. She's a real actress. Bottom line. And she is Susie Salmon. No one else could play her."

In the same 2009 *LA Times* article, another theme for Saoirse that still holds true was explored. Reporter Yvonne Villareal noted, "Ronan has avoided the flashbulb limelight that surround her young peers such as Miley Cyrus and Selena Gomez. And she doesn't expect that will change." Saoirse chimed in: "I don't think I would ever want fame like them. I have to say, I think Miley Cyrus is still quite young. She's what? Seventeen? I think she's very brave for all that fame to be thrown at her so young. She's like another Britney Spears. I don't envy her at all—or any of those girls who get that much attention. I suppose we're different kinds of actors. I focus on my work. The stuff that comes afterward—the press and premieres—it's fine, it's fun . . . but what I really want to do is work on my acting."

Saoirse speaking at *The Lovely Bones* press conference, New Zealand, 2009.

And in most respects—save going viral in ways she cannot control—what Saoirse predicted at age fifteen has not changed. More than a decade on, the same avoidance of the "flashbulb limelight" and resistance to too much tabloid attention remains the hallmark of Saoirse's public image.

> "I focus on my work. The stuff that comes afterward—the press and premieres—it's fine, it's fun . . . but what I really want to do is work on my acting."

Briony Tallis in *Atonement*

Briony's thorny complexity still sparks impassioned debate. Saoirse has maintained her own interpretations of the character since early days—and she'll still come to Briony's defense when the matter arises. *Backstage* writes of the young Saoirse at an *Atonement* screening: "[Saoirse] said her first reading of the script led her to believe Briony is a confused child rather than a vindictive brat who sets out to ruin someone's life. 'The main thing is that she's a storyteller,' said Ronan of her character."

The experience playing Briony was unique for many reasons, and particularly surreal because Saoirse had two accomplished performers, Romola Garai and Vanessa Redgrave, set to play Briony in the later stages of her life. In preparation for the shared role, they practiced mirroring Briony's mannerisms together. A choreographer was brought in to ensure the "continuity in their body movements" throughout the film. "It was a bit strange," Saoirse told *Backstage*. "We did little quirky things like that, because it's those kinds of little things that are [who] Briony is. She's kind of odd, I suppose."

Writing a profile of Saoirse for *The Lovely Bones* in *The Guardian*, Xan Brooks gets to the heart of the matter: "Ronan was so good in *Atonement*, arguably the best thing in it, because she gave us the sort of child rarely seen in films. Her Briony Tallis was neither a bad seed nor a clamoring cutey-pie. Instead, she was pensive, watchful, and complicated; wise beyond her years, though crucially not quite wise enough to read the nuances of adult sexuality."

Brooks related that Saoirse, now fifteen years old, was "annoyed" by those who still found Briony to be an unsympathetic character. "People say Briony's a bitch, and she's not," Saoirse said, leaping to her character's defense. "She's not vindictive or spiteful. It's just that she doesn't express her emotions; she just sits and observes everything." When asked, however, which character she herself was more like—Briony Tallis or Susie Salmon—Saoirse said that she was more of a Susie. "It wouldn't be healthy if I were like Briony."

Saoirse as Briony Tallis in *Atonement*, 2007.

chapter 3

A Maturing Range

"I think the miracle of Saoirse as an actor is that we watched her grow up, and every minute she is at her fullness."

—Greta Gerwig on Saoirse, 2020

In addition to *The Lovely Bones*, a stretch of Saoirse's career saw her take on a lead role in the fantasy adventure *City of Ember* (one of the few "kids' movies" she made in 2008), as well as an assortment of parts that established her versatility. She played a Polish orphan in the WWII drama *The Way Back* (2010) with Colin Farrell and Ed Harris, followed by not one but two stints as a teenage assassin within a year.

In *Hanna* (2011), where she reunited with *Atonement* director Joe Wright, Saoirse stars in the title role of a sixteen-year-old girl who is raised in the wilderness by her father (Eric Bana). Besides her father, Hanna has had no contact with the outside world. She has been taught

Saoirse at a press conference for *The Host*, 2013.

how to kill without mercy and has learned an impressive range of foreign languages and facts, but she knows little about modern society and human interaction. When danger encroaches, she sets out on her own, pursued by an even more ruthless force, Cate Blanchett as CIA agent Marissa Wiegler. Hanna gets a chance to see the world, though few who meet her along the way live to tell the tale.

The role required extensive fight training for Saoirse and saw her undertaking a new challenge as an action star. Wright was in on the action as well, helping to craft who Hanna was and how she moved, spoke, thought, and reacted alongside Saoirse. "We worked with [fight coordinator Jeff Imada] to create a very centered being, someone who stood grounded and balanced with a relaxed yet good posture. Hanna doesn't have the nervous twitches or slanted shoulders that come from years of social interaction. Her movements as Hanna are quite aerodynamic," Wright said, "though I was forever telling Saoirse to hold her elbows in when she ran; she has that natural tendency to flail them about."

In a very slight pivot, Saoirse was cast in *Violet & Daisy* (2011) where she played another ruthless teenage assassin. This time, she was paired up with Alexis Bledel, while James Gandolfini served as their target—though the film has a more comedic bent than *Hanna*. "I remember having a meeting with Geoffrey Fletcher, who directed *Violet & Daisy*, and I told him just my concern of playing an assassin twice in one year, you know? But I can promise you that *Violet & Daisy* is very, very different to *Hanna*. It's a black comedy and Daisy is definitely not a killer at all, so it was fine. The only similarity really between the two is they both hold guns," Saoirse told *Chicago Tribune*.

A FIERCELY INDEPENDENT BENT

While Saoirse's performances in this era were met with acclaim, and she demonstrated a jaw-dropping range, the films after *City of Ember* and *The Lovely Bones* were somewhat smaller in budget and box-office traction. They announced her commitment to independent cinema as well as experimental, boundary-pushing roles. She stayed true to a pursuit (perhaps begun in *Atonement*) of playing multifaceted women who refuse to compromise themselves. Throughout her formative years, she never took on the sort of "love interest" part that is, too frequently, the role left to a young woman after the hero, the villain, and the sidekicks gobble up all the air in a script. There are no passive characters where Saoirse is waiting to be rescued by a hero. This was purposeful and guided by Saoirse's own preferences.

Saoirse expressed a strong aversion to being typecast, telling *Time Out* in 2013, "The thing with me is, I'm very independent. I do want to do my own thing." When the reporter brings up "the E-word: ethereal," an adjective commonly used to describe her at the time, Saoirse was quick to object: "'Everyone thinks I'm ethereal. But I'm not like that, you know. I'm not ethereal,' she protests, then relents with a sigh: 'Well, I might have a little bit of that quality to me, that old soul thing, but I'm not ethereal. I wanted to play different girls. It sounds kind of simple

---

Saoirse in *Violet & Daisy*, 2011.

"The thing with me is, I'm very independent. I do want to do my own thing."

and a bit silly . . . but I wanted to play someone who says *fuck*. I wanted to play someone who had a temper, had an attitude, and is a bit of a bitch.'"

Time Out noted that Saoirse was, at that moment, within "that tricky transition from child star to grown-up actress," and that she had recently "got her first (onscreen) snog in the Stephenie Meyer adaptation *The Host*." But that was not quite accurate, as Saoirse's first kiss—both in "real" life and on-screen—was a quick buss when she was twelve years old, in her first movie *I Could Never Be Your Woman*. "I was like proper prude, as well; I was not ready to kiss a boy myself," she recalled for *W* Magazine years later. "I called [director] Amy [Heckerling] over and was like, 'Amy, come here. Can we just like discuss the logistics of this whole kissing scene?'"

Filming for *The Host* (2013) began mere months after the final movie in Stephenie Meyer's *Twilight* franchise, *Breaking Dawn - Part 2*, released. The craze for Meyer's young adult vampire-romance book series and their subsequent film adaptations was a globe-spanning sensation, with the movies grossing over $3 billion worldwide. Following it was *The Host*, a sci-fi tale with aliens instead of vampires. Like *Twilight, The Host*'s protagonist is a determined young woman who must find her way back to the only family she has left, while fighting against massively powerful and otherworldly forces. In the middle of it all, she finds herself in a love triangle between attractive, occasionally shirtless young men.

The science fiction–heavy concept calls for Saoirse to essentially play two roles, that of human Melanie in flashbacks and parasitic alien Wanderer in the present. And oftentimes both personalities emerge and struggle for dominance over her body within the same scene. Along with offering her first romantic lead role, Saoirse ably juggles

How That Hanna Kiss Happened

A moving moment in the film *Hanna* resulted from Saoirse's suggestion, as director Joe Wright explained. Hanna attaches herself to a British family who are on a camper-van holiday, and befriends their teenage daughter, Sophie (played by Jessica Barden). The worldly Sophie is at first put off by Hanna's strange behavior, but slowly the two grow closer. In a scene where Hanna and Sophie lie in bed together, sharing secrets, Sophie gives Hanna a friendship bracelet, and then Hanna leans over to give Sophie a gentle kiss that speaks of newfound closeness for them both.

Wright related how much his actors forged the way forward for their characters. "I would let Saoirse and Jessica take the lead; the kiss between them was suggested by Saoirse. She said she thought it was what Hanna would do. Saoirse and I also talked about how Hanna has no preconception of what is beautiful and what is ugly. Everything just is what it is; one of the core aspects for us, which Saoirse portrays beautifully, was that Hanna judges no one. That's anathema to most of us, as we are brought up and taught to constantly judge people, places, and things against ourselves, our aspirations, and our fears."

In the frenetic, mostly violent universe of *Hanna*, the exchange between Hanna and Sophie is one of the most intimate and character-building scenes, showing Hanna's emotional evolution, growing maturity, and capacity for friendship and love.

not one but two romances, as both Melanie and Wanderer fall in love with different men. The film also calls for intense action scenes and stunts, many of which Saoirse performed with the kind of dogged determination she applies to every aspect of her work.

Directed by *Gattaca*'s Andrew Niccol with a healthy $40 million production budget, *The Host* was set up to potentially become a broader movie franchise in the same vein as *Twilight* and the other dystopian-YA-novel-to-film adaptation that released while *The Host* was filming, *The Hunger Games*. But while Suzanne Collins's adaptation became a juggernaut at the box office and launched another pop cultural-phenom franchise, *The Host* stumbled out of the gate. The movie received negative critical reviews, holding a 10 percent rating on Rotten Tomatoes, and was largely passed over by audiences. The underwhelming performance at the box office and critical mauling meant that any potential for follow-ups was highly unlikely.

In an otherwise negative review of *The Host*, *New York Times* movie critic Manohla Dargis summed up exactly where Saoirse was at this moment in time: "Ms. Ronan keeps on trucking. With her clear, steady gaze and a physical bearing and gestural style that feel highly disciplined, she has always come across as preternaturally mature. There's an almost otherworldly aspect to her screen presence, partly due to her stillness and her own translucent eyes, which can suggest grave intensity or utter detachment. She may turn into another Cate Blanchett. For now, though, Ms. Ronan, who turns nineteen next month, just has to prove that she is smoothly transitioning to adulthood and ready for the corresponding roles, which, for a young woman in American movies means she has to demonstrate sex appeal and kiss some guys. Ms. Ronan does. She's ready."

Dargis had a prescient view of Saoirse's future—but even this clear-eyed take couldn't have predicted what the next few years would bring. Saoirse was entering into the grown-up stage of her movie career, a time when she would star in some of the most well-received and beloved movies in the history of cinema.

"There's an almost otherworldly aspect to her screen presence, partly due to her stillness and her own translucent eyes."

—Manohla Dargis on Saoirse, 2013

Diane Kruger and Saoirse in *The Host*, 2013.

Tony Revolori and Saoirse in *The Grand Budapest Hotel*, 2014.

THE WES ANDERSON EFFECT

When Saoirse Ronan went to shoot Wes Anderson's *The Grand Budapest Hotel*, it was a coming-of-age moment for her—the sort of turning point in a young person's life that she'd played many times before and would play again to even greater acclaim. She was nineteen when the movie began filming, and it was "her first job without her parents chaperoning," as *Time Out* phrased it. At the age that some teenagers are leaving home for university, Saoirse found herself on perhaps the most surreal "campus" imaginable.

(left to right) Ralph Fiennes, Saoirse, and Tony Revolori in *The Grand Budapest Hotel*, 2014.

Wes Anderson—the director known for his distinct aesthetic sensibilities and quirky, audacious films like *The Royal Tenenbaums, The Life Aquatic, The Darjeeling Limited*, and *Moonrise Kingdom*—also gave direction when it came to his cast's living arrangements. He had them all live together at the same hotel while shooting in Germany, the actors' real lives blurring with their fictional counterparts.

The Grand Budapest Hotel is a narrative told in fragments, with stories set in different time periods all leading back to the eponymous building in its title. Part slapstick comedy, part deeply resonant warning about the encroaching nature of fascism, the movie is regarded as one of Anderson's best, with *Far Out* magazine declaring in 2024 that it remains his "magnum opus." As is customary in Anderson productions, it features a large ensemble cast, this one led by Ralph Fiennes, and offers room for plenty of Anderson regulars.

Saoirse played Agatha, a good-natured and brave young woman who worked as an apprentice baker in the 1930s. While she is the love interest of Tony Revolori's "lobby boy" Zero, Agatha is anything but a passive role. Much of the plot is advanced by her ingenuity and unflappable resolve, as she bakes tools into sumptuous treats to be smuggled into prison to assist a prison break. She also sneaks around the hotel to retrieve a precious painting, undaunted by the fascist soldiers pursuing her.

In a typical Anderson quirk, Agatha has a birthmark in the shape of Mexico on her cheek, and an unexplained Irish accent. It was the first time that Saoirse got to use her own accent in a movie, a development that arose while hashing out the character with Anderson. The two tested out a variety of accents for Agatha, ranging from German to British to American, but nothing seemed to click. Then Anderson suggested that she try using her own accent, as Saoirse related to the website Den of Geek. "I did it, and it just felt right," she said. "In a way, for a smaller character in a film, there always needs to be something that brings it alive for you. For me, [it's usually about the] accent. With an Irish accent in particular, there's always a feistiness to who we are as people and a warmth, as well. I think Agatha has that to her. She's got this inner strength, but yet is very warm and loving, so I think it is the perfect accent for her."

As for how she got involved in an Anderson movie, it turned out that it was an opportunity Saoirse had long been hoping for. When it came around, however, she approached it with some trepidation. "When I heard [Anderson] was going to send me the script to read, I genuinely thought it was a joke or there was something more to it," Saoirse told

"In a way, for a smaller character in a film, there always needs to be something that brings it alive for you. For me, [it's usually about the] accent. With an Irish accent in particular, there's always a feistiness to who we are as people and a warmth, as well."

(left to right) Jeff Goldblum, Tony Revolori, Wes Anderson, Saoirse Ronan, and Jeremy Dawson during premiere of *The Grand Budapest Hotel*, 2014.

a roundtable of reporters upon the film's release, as reported by news agency UPI. "Because I really am a huge fan of his, and it was the first time I was such a massive fan of someone and wanted to work with them so much for quite a while, and then actually got to. So that was exciting to me."

Anderson's films are so precisely composed of art direction and acting style that they can be recognized from a distance. These idiosyncrasies would be unnerving for any first-time player, but Saoirse felt grounded by the comprehensiveness of Anderson's approach. She explained, "I was nervous about it because the style of acting he has in his films is so different and there is a theatrical element to it, a sort of dry humor that I think requires a perfect balance in every performance, and I was nervous about not being able to do that for Wes, but he was great. He guides everyone extremely well. He is very secure in his vision, and he is very comfortable with everything he does. He knows it is going to work. He knows his ideas will work and there is something reassuring about that when you have a birthmark in the shape of Mexico on your face."

Saoirse's confidence in Anderson was not misplaced. *The Grand Budapest Hotel* is a masterpiece that only seems to gather more appreciation and relevance as it ages. Critics and audiences were also on board when it bowed, with the movie becoming Anderson's most successful box-office hit and holding steady at 92 percent "fresh" on Rotten Tomatoes. *The New York Times* review sums up the film succinctly: "It's all a lot of fun, but it isn't only fun. Or rather, it's fun in the service of a subtle and sober argument." It was nominated for eleven Academy Awards and won four—for Original Score, Costume Design, Makeup and Hairstyling, and Production Design. The ensemble cast's performance was applauded, with Saoirse's name now mentioned in the same sentence as some of Hollywood's biggest stars.

Saoirse at *The Grand Budapest Hotel* premiere, New York, February 2014.

THE NEW COMING-OF-AGE QUEEN

In discussing *The Grand Budapest Hotel* with Den of Geek, Saoirse was asked about her upcoming projects. She related that she was set to appear in Ryan Gosling's directorial debut, *How to Catch a Monster* (later retitled *Lost River*), and then the family drama *Stockholm, Pennsylvania*. She added: "Then straight after, [I'm] doing a film called *Brooklyn,* which is an Irish film, and I am playing an Irish girl, so that's exciting."

She couldn't have known it in 2014, but *Brooklyn* would be the first in a string of three films that would place Saoirse firmly and resoundingly on the map. She had a long-expressed desire to play a genuinely Irish character, and she got her chance to do so with *Brooklyn*. The small independent film turned out to be massive, both in terms of success and the impact it made on her career.

"I didn't realize up to that moment that [Eilis] was Mum, that it was the journey she made. So this is more than a film to me."

Making the movie was significant for Saoirse on both a personal and professional level. The story at its heart mirrored her own experience. Like protagonist Eilis Lacey, on her own and launched into life on a different continent away from everything she knew, Saoirse explored the ups and downs of life on her own in New York City. And because she was representing a distinctly Irish perspective and an Irish immigrant experience that was an earlier echo of her own parents' journey, she felt increased pressure weighing on her performance.

In stark contrast to *The Grand Budapest Hotel,* with its revolving cast door of characters and frenetic action, *Brooklyn* feels like a movie almost entirely anchored by Saoirse standing still. The personal life parallels and pressures related to the performance came together in the end, as Saoirse told *The Boston Globe*. "An Irish journalist I've known from back home since I was a kid, Michael O'Doherty is his name, he said, 'This was the first time I saw your Mum on-screen.' And I just bawled. I didn't realize up to that moment that [Eilis] was Mum, that it was the journey she made. So this is more than a film to me."

Even in interviews conducted nearly a decade after the movie came out, the emotions are still close to the surface for Saoirse. She also considers *Brooklyn,* and its subsequent success, a true turning point

(left to right) Saoirse, Domhnall Gleeson, Eileen O'Higgins, and Peter Campion in *Brooklyn,* 2015.

in her life. Part of this propulsion into a new phase was due to director John Crowley (*Intermission, We Live In Time*). "I wanted to leave home but I was very homesick," she told the *LA Times* in 2024. "I found it really hard, but I didn't want to go back—it was literally *Brooklyn*. I hadn't had anyone push me in the way [Crowley] did before. He treated me like an adult actor and that took me a minute and left me with a bit of a bruise."

For the same 2024 piece, Crowley was full of praise for his leading lady. "It was like watching somebody going out on a tightrope," he said. "And she made it look easy. Of course, it's not easy. It cost her. But I think she felt that she was truthfully expressing something of herself in the role and that's why it yielded so beautifully in her hands." He felt that Saoirse didn't need any dialogue to bring her characters alive on camera. "She could have had a great career in silent movies. She just has an ability to express emotion, [even] if you turn the sound down, in a way that is magical to me still."

Critics and audiences agreed with Crowley's estimation. *Brooklyn* was a hit, grossing more than $60 million worldwide on a budget of $11 million. In Ireland, it enjoyed the largest opening of any Irish drama since 1996. The close-knit cast, which included Jim Broadbent, Eileen O'Higgins, Emory Cohen, Julie Walters, and Domhnall Gleeson, were widely lauded, and Saoirse earned the most rave reviews she had received to date.

On top of that all-important Oscar nomination for Best Actress—her first Oscar nomination for a lead role—she also picked up nominations for Best Actress from the Golden Globes, the Critics' Choice Awards, the BAFTAs, and the Screen Actors Guild. She also won Best Performance by an Actress in a British Independent Film from the British Independent Film Awards.

Although she did not win the Oscar for *Brooklyn*, it's hard to view that night as anything but triumphant. Saoirse arrived at the ceremony

---

Saoirse and director John Crowley attend FOX Golden Globe Awards Party, January 2016.

resplendent in a show-stopping emerald green Calvin Klein sequined gown, her hair in loose waves to her shoulders. The color had been chosen to celebrate Saoirse, Ireland, and, of course, *Brooklyn*. The dress, with its deep neckline and close-fitting cut, was equal parts elegant, daring, and definitely more of a grown-up image than she had projected in the past.

Saoirse's fashion choice was also an intentional nod to that first big red-carpet moment. Per *USA Today*, she wore a "grown-up" version of her debut *Atonement* Oscars dress. She was clearly feeling reminiscent that night as she walked the red carpet, saying, "When I was here before that was my very first awards show, which is incredible for it to be your first awards show."

Looking back from the space of years and subsequent triumphs, Saoirse's feelings where *Brooklyn* is concerned are definitive. "It ended up being such a special film for me to do. That film gets to me in a way that nothing else I've done has."

Saoirse at the 88th Annual Academy Awards, February 2016.

Left: Emory Cohen and Saoirse in *Brooklyn*, 2015.

Following: Saoirse poses for a photo while promoting the film *Brooklyn* at the 2015 Toronto International Film Festival.

"It ended up being such a special film for me to do. That film gets to me in a way that nothing else I've done has."

Hanna in *Hanna*

When Saoirse reunited with *Atonement* director Joe Wright to make *Hanna*, it was a very different role for her. Saoirse had to transform her body as well as evolve her approach as an actor.

It was the complexities and rigor involved in playing Hanna that drew her to the role in the first place. "I want all the roles that I play to hold challenges," Saoirse explained as part of an in-house promotional piece by Focus Features. "With lots of action and a layered character, *Hanna* had them for me. It's unlike any other drama that I've done."

Saoirse trained extensively to turn herself into a convincing teenage assassin. She worked one-on-one with the film's fight coordinator, Jeff Imada, for more than six weeks, with the training running "five, six hours a day—and she never complained," Imada said. "I sometimes had to tell her when to quit. She was determined to come across as Hanna. I was really impressed with her."

Costar Eric Bana was also impressed with Saoirse's dedication and how ably she managed the action-heavy training sequences between their characters. "It's often harder to fight with an actor than a stunt person," he said, but Saoirse was committed and engaged. "Our fight scenes were unique, with a father teaching a daughter and not just two people going after each other and one winning . . . I've worked with a lot of guys who are not as tough as Saoirse is."

In the end, Saoirse's appreciation for her character didn't spring from her ability to take out a roomful of armed men, but her curiosity and open-minded nature. "My favorite quality of hers is that she is non-judgmental; she shows an open mind to, and a fascination with, everything," Saoirse explained. "She's a bit of a freak. But I like that; I like freaks." In a separate interview, Wright affirmed that the feeling was mutual. "These are the characters Saoirse and I are drawn to, because we both feel like freaks. That's what binds us together."

Saoirse in *Hanna*, 2011.

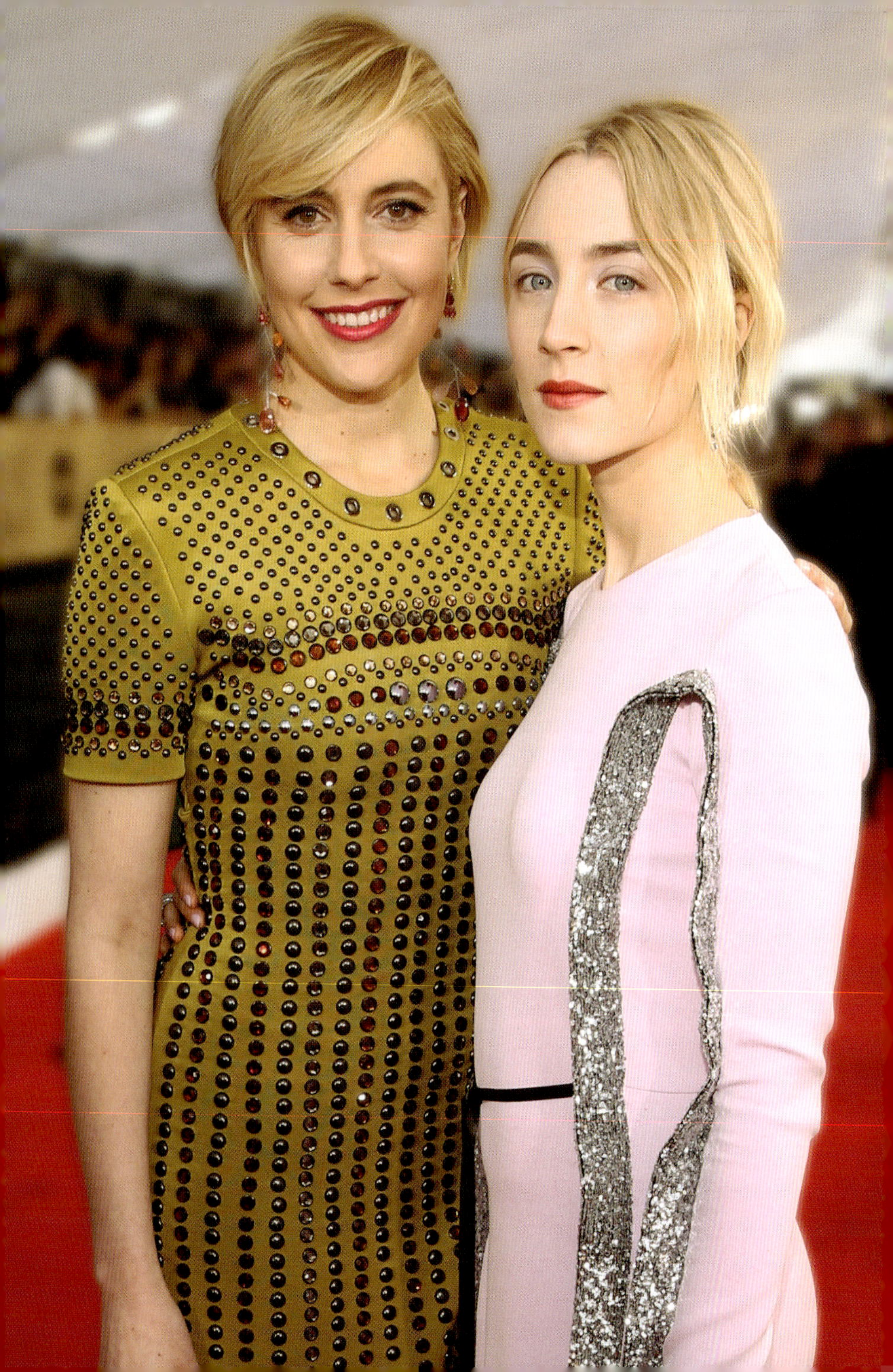

Chapter 4

The Making of a Dynamic Duo

"There's something about Saoirse onscreen. You feel like you could look straight through her, like you can see her insides and her brain working. I want an actress to feel like she's in full possession of the character–not like you're lending it to them, but that they own it."

—Greta Gerwig on *Lady Bird*

There was someone watching the 2016 Academy Awards at home who took note of the green *Brooklyn* dress. She and Saoirse already got on rather famously; she was rooting for Saoirse to win. And then they were going to make a movie together.

"I remember watching Saoirse, because every year I throw an Academy Awards party," director Greta Gerwig recalled in a joint *LA Times* interview with Saoirse in 2018. Gerwig had not yet attended

Greta Gerwig and Saoirse at the 24th Annual Screen Actors Guild Awards in Los Angeles, January 2018.

an Oscars ceremony herself. "So, I was watching Saoirse, who was so brilliant in *Brooklyn*, walk the red carpet . . . And I remember screaming, 'Noah [Baumbach, Gerwig's partner]! Tape the preshow!' And he was like, 'Oh God, this is going to go on forever.' But I watch all the interviews. And you said you wore your green dress for Ireland, and it was your good luck charm, and I was thinking, 'She's the best in the world! And she's in my movie!'"

Saoirse first met the actress-turned-director in person in 2015, when Gerwig dropped by Saoirse's hotel room at the Toronto Film Festival. The two had met virtually in the months prior and knew they had a promising connection. "I remember coming off that Skype call and I was like, 'Jesus Christ, I haven't felt that alive since I was fifteen years old!'" Saoirse recalled in the *LA Times* interview with Gerwig. The feeling was mutual. Gerwig added, "I felt like I knew you instantly. Like not just know you, but have you in my heart."

Saoirse and Greta Gerwig attend the 90th Annual Academy Awards Nominee Luncheon, California, February 2018.

"I remember coming off that Skype call and I was like, 'Jesus Christ, I haven't felt that alive since I was fifteen years old!'"

Meeting face-to-face confirmed that not only did they understand each other, they were more than keen to work together. "When we saw each other for the first time, it was exactly the same thing. She was doing *20th Century Women*, and I was in Toronto [premiering *Brooklyn*], and she flew in to see me," Saoirse related to *The Hollywood Reporter*. "It was late at night, and I was nervous because . . . it was her!"

Gerwig, who had begun her career in acting and established herself as the queen of "mumblecore" movies before making the leap to directing and screenwriting, was as enthusiastic. She was finally in the same room with the actor she wanted at the heart of her film.

"Saoirse opened the door with a Coca-Cola and her slippers," she recalled to the *LA Times*. "Just a regular Coke. I thought, 'I like this girl.'" By all accounts, after this promising meet-cute, the two got on like a house on fire. And they quickly got down to business. The *LA Times* wrote: "Ronan also had some French onion soup that she ordered from room service, but she never removed the protective cellophane covering the bowl because for the next couple of hours, the two women did nothing but read the script, laugh, cry, bond, and yes, share a few more (soft) drinks of the non-diet variety."

A LADY BIRD IS BORN

The script they read that day in Saoirse's hotel room was for *Lady Bird*, which Gerwig had written and was slated to direct—her first undertaking as a writer-director.

Lady Bird navigates the hallmarks of American coming-of-age narratives—first loves, romantic betrayal, conflicts with friends, trouble in school, raucous house parties, sexual misadventures, questions of identity and belonging—yet keeps as its core an emphasis on a tense mother-daughter dynamic that feels unflinching and real. Lady Bird and her mother, Marion (played by Laurie Metcalf), love each other, but they also know just how to push the buttons to wound each other. The movie opens memorably, with Lady Bird flinging herself out of a moving car and breaking her arm to escape Marion's lecturing.

Saoirse in *Lady Bird*, 2017.

"I really identify with that juxtaposition of confidence and insecurity and how you can really believe in yourself but not quite know exactly what you believe in."

Saoirse, who maintains a fantastically close relationship with her mother, Monica, still found much that called to her in Gerwig's script. "*Lady Bird* shows the beauty and the frustration of being a teenager, especially around that age when you're just about to leave home and you just want to get out of the place where you grew up," she told *The Hollywood Reporter*. "I really identify with that juxtaposition of confidence and insecurity and how you can really believe in yourself but not quite know exactly what you believe in."

Gerwig assembled a cast of veteran actors and on-the-rise young stars around her leading lady. In addition to Metcalf—a dynamic presence in film, TV, and theater since the 1970s—Tracy Letts, one of America's greatest living playwrights, was Lady Bird's more easy-going father, who is increasingly downtrodden by his unemployed state. Then there was Timothée Chalamet, whose career would explode with *Lady Bird*'s release in 2017 alongside his Oscar-nominated work in *Call Me by Your Name*. Chalamet played one of Lady Bird's love interests, the popular, wealthy, aloof Kyle; while Beanie Feldstein played Lady Bird's

"I told her, 'Wait until you're with me to watch it so we can cry together.'"

straight-and-narrow best friend, Julie; and Lucas Hedges took on the role of Lady Bird's first boyfriend, Danny—an idyllic-seeming teenage dream of a relationship until it's not.

To prepare to play a distinctly American sort of teenager at a distinct time of life, Saoirse relied on knowledge she had gleaned from TV series and movies from her own teenage years as well as by watching newer shows for an updated view. "One thing that definitely exists in the States more so than in Ireland is the popular crowd, and the need to fit in with whoever is considered popular," Saoirse told *Vanity Fair*. "That's something we don't really have as much of, or at least to that extreme, in Ireland. That was something the shows I watched—like *Sabrina the Teenage Witch*, *That's So Raven*, and *Lizzie McGuire*—taught me."

Gerwig also had her watch "John Hughes coming-of-age classics," *Pretty in Pink* and *Sixteen Candles* amongst them, for a thorough grounding in Lady Bird's motivations. These films would help "get an understanding of the way Lady Bird wants her life to pan out," Saoirse explained. "Greta put it really well to me. She said that the movie Lady Bird sees in her head is not the movie that we're all watching. It was good to be aware of the romanticism around being a teenager and falling in love and finding yourself."

Lady Bird also had an even broader market, and it sparked a far-reaching cultural conversation about the relationship between mothers and daughters. Saoirse looked forward to sharing the movie with her own mother, even asking her not to watch the film until they saw it together. "I just really want[ed] to watch it with her," she told *Vanity Fair*. "I told her, 'Wait until you're with me to watch it so we can cry together.'"

Saoirse in *Lady Bird*, 2017.

A GOLDEN EVENING

All the meticulous planning and obvious labors of love that went into *Lady Bird* came to fruition upon the film's release. Critics went into ecstasy over it, with audiences not far behind. The movie broke Rotten Tomatoes's records with high scores returned across the board and quickly became a buzzed-about Oscar frontrunner.

The New York Times said that Lady Bird was "played with daunting, dauntless precision by Saoirse Ronan (already, at twenty-three, one of the most formidable actors in movies today)" while Susan Wloszczyna, writing for RogerEbert.com, wrote: "Of course, the MVP here is Ronan, whose Lady Bird is as far from her sweet Irish lass in *Brooklyn* as she can be. Bedecked with a messy blood-red dye job, a smattering of acne and thrift-shop chic sensibilities, she is thoughtful and impulsive, sharp and naïve in equal measure." *The Guardian* especially highlighted the mother-daughter push and pull, noting that the "scenes between Ronan and Metcalf are electric." *Empire Online* declared, "A coming-of-age story like no other, Lady Bird is smart, emotional, funny, and completely original. Rarely has a directorial debut been so assured, so singular and so heartwarmingly affecting."

It would be Gerwig's writing and direction, and the acting turns from Saoirse and Metcalf, that caught the movie industry's attention. *Lady Bird* was a darling of the awards season, and at the 75th Golden Globe Awards in 2018, it was nominated four times and won two of the

"Of course, the MVP here is Ronan, whose Lady Bird is as far from her sweet Irish lass in *Brooklyn* as she can be."

—Susan Wloszczyna on Saoirse, 2017

Greta Gerwig and Saoirse pose with the award for Best Motion Picture Musical or Comedy for *Lady Bird* at the 75th Annual Golden Globe Awards, January 2018.

night's biggest: Best Motion Picture—Musical or Comedy and Best Actress—Musical or Comedy for Saoirse. After years of not taking home a trophy, the Best Acting accolade was finally hers.

When she went to claim her long-deserved statuette, there was another woman she was eager to share the win with. "Oh, thank you!" Saoirse exclaimed at the start of her speech. "My mum's on FaceTime over on someone's phone! So, hi!" After this shout-out to Monica Ronan—so instrumental in her life and career—she then extended her circle of love and excitement: "I have no time at all to say thank you, but I just want to say how inspirational it's been to be in this room tonight. I'm here with my best friend, Eileen [O'Higgins]. I just want to thank HFPA [The Hollywood Foreign Press Association] for the award, A24, Greta, all the producers on the film. All of the women who I love so much in my own life who support me every single day."

Although Saoirse, Gerwig, and Metcalf would also find themselves nominated that year at the Oscars, that night did not prove as magical for *Lady Bird*. The Academy tends to favor drama over comedy, and in 2018 they gave Best Picture to Guillermo Del Toro's *The Shape of Water*, while Frances McDormand won Best Actress for *Three Billboards Outside Ebbing, Missouri*.

For the Oscars ceremony, in contrast to the Globes, Saoirse wore a candy-pink confection of a Calvin Klein dress, strapless, with a voluminous bow and train. "It's a color we hadn't done," stylist Elizabeth Saltzman told *Women's Wear Daily*. "This time, this is about the woman herself. She's already flying a flag for her country, so we decided to stay away from dark." When they'd been choosing between two dresses, it was Saoirse's reaction that made the choice clear. "There was a clear, right moment," Saltzman went on. "There was a lot of emotion. It was genuine, deep happiness. Huge grin, that beautiful Saoirse calm, peaceful exuberance. It's exactly what you want a woman to feel like."

Saoirse at the 90th Annual Academy Awards, March 2018.

LEVELING UP

Following the enormous success of *Lady Bird* and the profound bond that had been forged between the director and her leading lady, it was only a matter of time before Gerwig and Saoirse teamed up again. They would reunite within the space of a year, in fact, to start filming *Little Women,* Gerwig's refreshed take on Louisa May Alcott's beloved novel.

In between, however, Saoirse had other significant projects simmering. She starred opposite Billy Howle in director Dominic Cooke's *On Chesil Beach,* an adaptation of Ian McEwan's novel, breathing life into another McEwan protagonist ten years after Briony Tallis in *Atonement*. She also appeared in director Michael Mayer's film *The Seagull,* adapted from the play by Anton Chekhov. There she plays the ingenue role, Nina, with Howle once more at her side as her lover Konstantin, in a cast that also features Annette Bening, Elisabeth Moss, and Corey Stoll. And in 2018, a movie that Saoirse had long been attached to finally hit screens. In *Mary Queen of Scots* she takes up the royal mantle as the titular queen, proud and determined to raise Scotland to glory and challenge the primacy of her cousin, England's Queen Elizabeth I.

Mary Queen of Scots was a movie plagued by what Hollywood likes to call "development hell" practically since its inception. In 2007, Scarlett Johansson was attached to the title role. In 2012, when she was eighteen, Saoirse was announced as Mary, but it took another

"Saoirse Ronan's face looms out of the screen in this period movie like the figurehead on a warship's prow: fierce, sharp, defiant."

—*The Guardian* on *Mary Queen of Scots,* 2019

Saoirse in *Mary Queen of Scots*, 2018.

half-decade for Margot Robbie to be cast as Elizabeth. Despite the stop-starts of its development, the film finalized an all-star supporting cast, including Guy Pearce, David Tennant, Jack Lowden, Gemma Chan, Joe Alywn, and James McArdle.

In their review, *The Guardian* wrote that Saoirse plays the legendary Mary with panache: "Saoirse Ronan's face looms out of the screen in this period movie like the figurehead on a warship's prow: fierce, sharp, defiant. She inhabits the persona of Mary Stuart so utterly that it took me a moment to remember that it was this same performer who only last year was starring in *Lady Bird*, a modern-day teen at war with her mum" and that "Ronan is just so good in this movie—so intelligent, so passionate."

On the whole, critics were divided about the film, but once again, Saoirse's phenomenal range was on full display. She plays Mary in several stages of her life, from a young, sheltered royal through mounting betrayals and personal horrors. She makes love on screen, gives birth, suffers through assault, finally encounters her royal rival, and, at the last, kneels to be beheaded with unyielding dignity. Though she had played characters from many historical eras before, *Mary* has an epic sweep and scope that feels new. It's not hard to imagine that with a somewhat different script, it would have become a confident awards contender.

FROM SCOTLAND TO CONCORD, MASSACHUSETTS

Saoirse's experience playing the lead—and a queen—in *Mary* allowed her to approach *Little Women* with even more confidence. "I'd had the experience of making *Brooklyn* and *Lady Bird* that was quite chaotic for me in my head," Saoirse told *USA Today* in 2024, looking back at this transformative period of her life. "I felt very overwhelmed and self-conscious, and luckily, I had two brilliant directors who knew how to use whatever messy, emotional state I was in to make something coherent." Stepping into Mary's shoes meant treading a different path,

(left to right) Emma Watson, Saoirse, Florence Pugh, and Eliza Scanlen in *Little Women*, 2019.
Following: Saoirse in *Little Women*, 2019.

as embodying a character in "the ultimate position of power . . . gave me a bit more confidence that I feel like I'd lost for a while. By the time I made *Little Women*, I felt very in my power. I wasn't afraid to make mistakes or fall on my face."

Little Women has been a hot property since it was first published in 1868. The story hardly lacks adaptations, first set to film as a silent drama in 1917. Yet it now seems fitting that every generation have its go-to *Little Women* movie. Gerwig would have grown up with the 1994 movie directed by Gillian Armstrong that featured Winona Ryder as Jo. Armstrong's take was beloved, but Gerwig was determined to make her own *Little Women* for a new age and new viewers.

As NPR put it in an interview with Gerwig, "This latest version

"By the time I made *Little Women*, I felt very in my **power**. I wasn't afraid to make **mistakes** or fall on **my face.**"

comes from another young woman who, like Louisa May Alcott, has captured the sensibilities of the young women of her time." Gerwig expressed a keen sense of inspiration from protagonist Jo March. "I don't remember when I first encountered [*Little Women*]. I don't remember a time when I didn't know who Jo March was," she said.

In Gerwig's adaptation, the focus stays on her beloved Jo, but she also frames Jo in a new light, zooming in on Jo's writerly ambitions and her triumph therein. Less vital is the romantic storyline that Alcott was made to serve as the conclusion for *her* Jo's more traditional narrative.

Casting Jo would be the lynchpin for Gerwig, but surprisingly, she did not initially picture Lady Bird as her leading lady. It was Saoirse who informed Gerwig that she would be playing the part, in a development that seemed to astonish them both. As Gerwig told *Vanity Fair*: "Actually, Saoirse told me she was going to play Jo. She knew I was working on it,

(left to right) Emma Watson, Florence Pugh, Saoirse Ronan, and Eliza Scanlen in character as the March sisters in *Little Women*, 2019.

and she said, 'I know your goal, you're writing it. I know you're writing, and I'm going to play Jo.' . . . And it felt like a very Jo thing to do, to kind of claim her space. And she told me later she's never done anything like that, and she's never done anything like that again."

Saoirse also felt a keen sense of connection to her famous character. Jo's intrepid ambition called to mind her own unswerving nature. Perhaps it was this alignment with the spirited Jo that prompted her to so boldly claim the part. "We're both pigheaded, I think. Jo and I are both stubborn," she told *The Jakarta Post*. "You see in the earlier part of the film where she drags all her sisters and their friend Hannah to be a part of her play that she's written. She spent all night going over the scenes. I used to do that when I was younger. I'd force my friends to make a little short film with me. None of them enjoyed it, but I did because I was in charge."

(left to right) Florence Pugh, Saoirse Ronan, and Emma Watson in *Little Women*, 2019.

Following: Saoirse and Timothée Chalamet in *Little Women*, 2019.

"There's a real sort of like aliveness I think, when I work with Timothée. That's how I feel."

Saoirse and Greta Gerwig on set during the making of the 2019 film *Little Women.*

Opposite: Saoirse, Laura Dern, Eliza Scanlen, Emma Watson, and Florence Pugh in *Little Women*, 2019.

Production commenced with an all-star cast. Following Gerwig's success with *Lady Bird* and the reputation that she had established as an actor in Hollywood, many were eager to work on the project. Also returning from *Lady Bird* was Timothée Chalamet as Laurie, Jo's best friend and would-be love interest. It would mark the second collaboration for Chalamet and Saoirse, whose on-screen chemistry and offscreen friendship was celebrated by critics and fans alike. "We've obviously gone off to make other projects away from each other, but I've not really had an experience acting with anyone else like I have done with you," Saoirse said in a 2025 conversation with Chalamet. "There's a real sort of like aliveness I think, when I work with Timothée. That's how I feel."

On Set with Meryl Streep

Though she only shared one major scene with Streep in *Little Women*, Saoirse was over the moon to be acting alongside a living legend. Streep has long been considered one of the best actresses that modern cinema has produced, and throughout her career, Saoirse was compared to her or referred to as a young Streep-in-the-making in glowing profiles (and by Ryan Gosling).

When filming, Saoirse was determined to be a consummate professional, as she related on *The Ellen DeGeneres Show*. "I was like, 'It's going to be great and it's going to be lovely to have this one scene with her' and it was," Saoirse said. "We did it and I kind of kept my cool because I had to, and we needed to make sure the scene was just right."

Only once the work was done did she let herself indulge in the enormity of the collaboration. "When they called 'cut' on the last setup and they were going to check it and move on, suddenly I was like, 'Oh my god, I got to work with Meryl Streep,' and it all sort of hit me then." She offered further details in an appearance on *Late Night With Seth Meyers*, joking that she pressed Streep into an embrace. "I got really emotional, and I was just thanking her for letting me act and stuff. I just sort of held her and not let her go. I basically forced her into a hug and just said thank you."

(left to right) Meryl Streep, Florence Pugh, Greta Gerwig, Saoirse Ronan, and Laura Dern at a special film screening of *Little Women* at the DGA in California, October 2019.

It wasn't the first hug between them. Speaking to *The Jakarta Post* after the filming of *Little Women*, Saoirse recalled a much earlier encounter, when she was "no one." "I met Meryl a few years ago with Stanley Tucci, who's done many films with her . . . we were at an awards show. I was fifteen. *The Devil Wears Prada* had come out. I turned to Stanley, and I was [like], 'Oh my God, I can't believe Meryl's here.' He said, 'Come on, we'll go meet her.' So, I met her, and she was so lovely. She gave me the biggest hug. I was no one. I was just some random actress."

Tracy Letts also returned to play Mr. Dashwood. Rounding out the March family was Florence Pugh as free-spirited Amy, Emma Watson as the more conventional Meg, Eliza Scanlen as gentle, doomed Beth, Laura Dern as mother Marmee, and Bob Odenkirk as Father March. In a particular coup of casting, Meryl Streep played the sharp-tongued, ever-judgmental Aunt March.

Saoirse discussed how playing Jo March was a transformative experience, in an interview with *The Jakarta Post*. "I do feel it has changed me. I feel [it] definitely as an actor [and] getting the chance to play somebody who just gave me the license to do anything." Stepping into Jo's feisty, fiery, and ambitious shoes was empowering for Saoirse, and extended into her own approach to acting. "I'm a real perfectionist about things, but it was the first time ever that I was on a job where . . . [I told myself] I'm going to try something, and I might mess it up, and it might not be right, but I want to try it. I've never had the guts to do that before to that extent."

Once again, audiences and critics loved the synergy that Saoirse and Gerwig cooked up between them. *Little Women* was a box-office hit and reviews were resoundingly positive. Particular praise was heaped upon the performances, direction, and Gerwig's script. The inclusion of more modern themes, especially a refreshed ending for Jo that put more emphasis on her literary achievements than her romantic side plot, and Gerwig's decision to use some of Alcott's diary entries and other writings as dialogue, were lauded. *USA Today* said that the script "makes Alcott's time and language feel effervescently modern and authentically nostalgic," and it has since been added to the Writers Guild of America's "101 Greatest Screenplays of the 21st Century (So Far)."

At the Oscars, the movie was nominated for Best Picture, Best Actress for Saoirse, Best Supporting Actress for Florence Pugh, Best Adapted Screenplay for Gerwig, and Best Original Score; it won Best Costume Design. Considering the film was so celebrated and so highly nominated, there was some pushback that Gerwig did not earn a Best Director nod as she had for *Lady Bird*. Gerwig publicly took this in

> "I'm a real perfectionist about things, but it was the first time ever that I was on a job where . . . [I told myself] I'm going to try something, and I might mess it up, and it might not be right, but I want to try it. I've never had the guts to do that before to that extent."

stride, releasing a warm statement that thanked the entirety of *Little Women*'s cast, crew, and creatives, in which she referred to Saoirse as her "filmmaking partner/wizard/genius" and added, "You are my inspiration and my honesty and my cocaptain, always." Gerwig's career would be headed to unimaginably higher heights, with the record-shattering *Barbie* on the horizon.

Christine "Lady Bird" McPherson in *Lady Bird*

Even though there are many elements from director Greta Gerwig's own Sacramento adolescence infused throughout *Lady Bird*, the story is not biographical, and Gerwig insists that she was nothing like Lady Bird growing up. Both the character and the director are Sacramento natives, attended an all-girl Catholic high school, and left California for an East Coast college experience. But Gerwig has said the similarities stop there.

"I was actually sort of the opposite of Lady Bird," Gerwig said in a conversation with NPR's Audie Cornish on *All Things Considered*. "The movie—I always say it's not true, but it rhymes with the truth."

Lady Bird is a unique and compelling character, of a sort rarely represented in movies about American teenagers, let alone teenage girls. It's possible cinema had never seen her like that before. She is clever, stubborn, self-destructive, independent, and ferociously uncompromising. She is guided by her impulses and often acts without thinking or caring about the consequences. She is unapologetically herself while at the same time engaged in a frantic pursuit of uncovering who she wants to be.

This complexity and variability of character both attracted Saoirse to the part and made her nervous about pulling it off. As she explained to *Variety* in a joint cover story with Gerwig, "What I knew would be so exciting about playing her and what was also really scary about playing her, is that she's sort of trying on all these different roles, to see which one fits best . . . She's testing them all out. She's testing herself all the time."

Both Gerwig and Saoirse have received feedback directly from the people that *Lady Bird* was made for—and made to reflect. "A lot of women have told me, particularly women who are in their 50s or 60s—they've said, you know, I've been that mother, and I've been that daughter, and I understand both," Gerwig said. As for Saoirse: "I've had girls, really smart girls, come up to me, and they're so excited that they've finally got their movie. A lot of them say, 'That was me! I was Lady Bird.'"

Beanie Feldstein and Saoirse in an emotional scene in *Lady Bird*, 2017.

GORILLAZ

chapter 5

Connecting with Costars and Directors

"I don't want to imagine you making a film without me! I can't stand it!"

—Saoirse on Greta Gerwig

Over the years, Saoirse has returned to work again and again with several creatives, speaking to the special relationships that evolved between them. But one connection stands out in particular. Saoirse and director Greta Gerwig seem like an unshakable duo following the success of their popular and well-received collaborations on *Lady Bird* and *Little Women*. The association between Gerwig and Saoirse is so intensely entwined that it's all but assumed Saoirse is at the top of Gerwig's go-to list, no matter the project.

With their effusive friendship, often on display at press events and in media profiles, Gerwig and Saoirse further cemented their connection for both peers and audiences alike. They've been forthright

---

Timothée Chalamet and Saoirse pose at a morning photocall for *Little Women* at the Corinthia Hotel in London, December 2019.

about wanting to work together as much as possible, for as long as possible. "I hope we get to be old ladies together making movies about old ladies," Gerwig said in a shared *The Hollywood Reporter* interview. She went on to explain that as close as the two had grown during *Lady Bird*, taking on *Little Women* together was a different affair—because this time, their familiarity inspired a unique collaboration that shaped many aspects of the movie.

Saoirse's presence has been known to inform many elements of Gerwig's filmmaking process, with Gerwig expressing that Saoirse was a "second director" on *Little Women*. "It's the benefit of working with someone you've worked with before," Gerwig said. "I felt like, in some ways, I had conceived *Lady Bird* before I knew she was playing it. And I had written my drafts of *Little Women* before I knew she was playing it. But I don't know any other way to say it except she was an author of *Lady Bird*, but even more so she was an author of *Little Women*. I felt like she knew exactly what we were making the whole time as a filmmaker, as much as an actor. She really became a second director for me. It was like an extension of every thought I had; she'd walk it out another step." Saoirse was in full agreement. "There's no other working relationship I have like the one I have with Greta."

If Saoirse ends up helming her own projects, there will be a direct line to her experiences with Gerwig. When *The Hollywood Reporter* asked during their interview, "Saoirse, after watching Greta, do you ever think about writing or directing?" Gerwig was the first to respond, with an enthusiastic and encouraging, "Hell yes, she does!"

The topic had clearly been discussed between them before, with Gerwig fully behind such next steps for her star. Saoirse was also quick to answer after Gerwig's affirmation. "I think working with Greta over the past few years really allowed me to seriously consider doing it in a way that I haven't before," she said, then went on to reveal how observing Gerwig at work in such a traditionally male-dominated field has encouraged her. "I do think that even though I don't see Greta as a 'woman director'—she's just a brilliant director—there is definitely

Greta Gerwig and Saoirse at the Film Independent Spirit Awards in California, March 2018.

> "Seeing her take on that role as the captain of the ship, and do it so beautifully, has been an inspiration."
>
> —Saoirse on Gerwig

something about seeing a woman that you're close to and feel a kinship with do what she's doing and have that authority on a film. Seeing her take on that role as the captain of the ship, and do it so beautifully, has been an inspiration."

With sentiments like these, it's no surprise that other actors and directors in Hollywood expect that Saoirse will always be part of Gerwig's thought process when plotting out her upcoming projects. And who knows what the future holds—perhaps Saoirse will try her hand at directing and persuade Gerwig to return to her acting roots in what would be a lovely reversal of roles for them both.

Greta Gerwig and Saoirse at the Film Independent Spirit Awards, 2018.

Following: Greta Gerwig and Saoirse at The BAFTA Los Angeles Tea Party at Four Seasons Hotel, January 2020.

CINEMA SOULMATES

Considering their unwavering closeness, it came as a surprise when Saoirse did not appear in Gerwig's *Barbie* (2023), the director's biggest film to date and a roaring box-office success. *Barbie* featured Saoirse's *Mary Queen of Scots* costar Margot Robbie in the role of the world's most famous doll, and it was a pop-culture sensation as well as a smash hit with audiences. Gerwig became the first female director to helm a movie that raked in more than a billion dollars at the box office, breaking records and breaking down barriers.

It turns out that Saoirse *was* set to appear, but scheduling conflicts got in the way. "There was a whole character I was going to play—another Barbie," Saoirse explained, as reported by the *Independent*. "I was gutted I couldn't do it." She went on to say that she wanted so badly to be a part of the movie that she'd texted Gerwig and Robbie that she was up for anything: "I'm like, 'If you're doing any pick-up [shots], maybe I can just walk through the background?'" But commitments for Saoirse's shoot on *The Outrun* wouldn't allow it in the end, though she revealed more about the character Gerwig had envisioned for her. "I was definitely going to be a Weird Barbie," Saoirse told *Variety*, a part that would have seen her as an outside-the-norm Barbie alongside comedian Kate McKinnon, who played the film's primary "Weird Barbie." Saoirse then joked, "I don't know how to take that."

Gerwig had in fact hoped that two of her longest-running collaborators—and biggest stars—would show up in *Barbie*. She envisioned both Saoirse and her *Lady Bird* and *Little Women* costar Timothée Chalamet making "specialty cameos." Chalamet confirmed this, relating in an appearance on *The Tonight Show Starring Jimmy Fallon*, "There was an idea for Saoirse Ronan and I to do a cameo in it. I don't know what the cameo would've been. I think it would've been one of the rejected Kens or Barbies—not Allan. Maybe there was a reject French one along the way."

That Gerwig had wanted a Saoirse and Chalamet cameo, and perhaps even pitched them on it together, is understandable. The close

"I was definitely going to be a Weird Barbie . . . I don't know how to take that."

friendship and ongoing professional relationship that evolved between her two young stars is often on exuberant display, like the Saoirse/Gerwig bond.

Vogue described Saoirse and Chalamet as "cinema soulmates," and their collaborations have extended beyond the Greta-verse. At a special 2024 event for *Vanity Fair* called "Reunited Live," in which the magazine brought together Oscar contenders who have previously worked together, Saoirse and Chalamet spoke about the chemistry they discovered on-screen, which has been further fueled by a genuine attachment formed when the cameras stopped rolling.

At the sold-out event, Chalamet recalled the first time they met in the run-up to *Lady Bird*. "We had this rehearsal with Greta and—I am going to do a lot of blowing smoke tonight, so just get ready—Saoirse continues to be a legend, but already she was a legend then. I was just blown away immediately just by her level of talent." Saoirse followed that up: "We were very lucky that we clicked straight away, and we had Greta, who was so excited by whatever was happening between the two of us."

Chalamet, who is American and French and grew up spending time in both countries, is now one of the most in-demand actors in Hollywood. He has headlined big-budget cinematic events like *Dune*

"Saoirse continues to be a legend, but already she was a legend then. I was just blown away immediately just by her level of talent."

—Timothée on Saoirse, 2024

Timothée Chalamet and Saoirse onstage at the 33rd Santa Barbara International Film Festival at Arlington Theatre, February 2018.

and *Wonka*, and given award-winning, character-driven turns like his performance as Bob Dylan in the biopic *A Complete Unknown*. But when he and Saoirse first met, his own acting experiences were more limited than hers, leading him to regard her as a "legend" on the *Lady Bird* set. They quickly became close, sharing honest conversations, developing real trust, and forming the kind of rapport that makes their performances together feel both electric and authentic.

"I felt really relieved to have you there," Saoirse remembered of their time on *Lady Bird* at "Reunited Live." "Having someone who had this sort of European flair in the way that you did, and you were so sort of unique and nothing I'd ever met before—that was really refreshing for me." After she praised his work in *A Complete Unknown*, Chalamet made it clear just how profound their relationship remains, naming Saoirse akin to family. "To hear my sister, in many ways, commend that, it is really moving to me," he replied.

THE CHOSEN WRITERS AND DIRECTORS

Chalamet and Saoirse appeared in their third shared film in 2021 for Wes Anderson's comedy-drama *The French Dispatch*. A sprawling movie with a massive ensemble cast, told anthology-style in distinct parts, the two don't appear in any scenes together. But the fact of their "reunion" was an angle used widely in the press when covering the film's development—showing that they remain entwined in public perception. Working on *The French Dispatch* also meant that Saoirse was teaming up again with Anderson, and after *The Grand Budapest Hotel* could now be credited as one of his "regulars." She was on an eye-popping cast list that also included her *Budapest* costars Adrien Brody, Bill Murray, Tilda Swinton, Léa Seydoux, Edward Norton, Willem Dafoe, Jason Schwartzman, Tony Revolori, and Owen Wilson.

Saoirse was keen to jump on board an Anderson project once more, this time in a small role as part of a much larger whole. "I just love being a part of anything [Anderson's] doing, really, because you always know it's gonna be good," she told Collider. "You're not going, 'I wonder if people will like this?' They always do. And it never really gets old. It's a real event when people go see a Wes Anderson film." The betting odds are extremely good that we'll see Saoirse in upcoming Anderson productions as well, considering that the enthusiasm and admiration between star and director appears to be mutual.

"I could tell that Wes was not 100 percent thrilled that I was working with her," Greta Gerwig related to *The Hollywood Reporter*. "He loves her. I remember I asked Wes about Saoirse. He read the script [for *Lady Bird*] and was like, 'Saoirse can do anything. She can do absolutely anything.' I may be projecting, but I think he might've been a little jealous because he's trying to take her back." Gerwig laughed, adding, "We're in a round robin with Joe Wright."

Joe Wright, Saoirse's director on *Atonement* and the man who had helped launch her into stardom, is another trusted collaborator. Saoirse

Saoirse and Winsen Ait Hellal in *The French Dispatch*, 2021.

"I just love being a part of anything [Anderson's] doing, really, because you always know it's gonna be good."

Saoirse and director Joe Wright at the after party for the New York screening of *Hanna*, April 2011.

"Because my safety net was, you can just put the camera on Saoirse in close-up–what she's thinking–and that will see you through a scene."

—Joe Wright on Saoirse

teamed up with him again on *Hanna* when she was sixteen. By this point, she had become such a force of nature in Hollywood that she was the one who was able to suggest Wright's involvement in the movie, rather than the other way around.

Wright went into further detail about the collaborative nature of their relationship: the trust they share, and how central Saoirse's involvement was in his agreeing to make *Hanna*. "The real deal-breaker was Saoirse; if she hadn't been involved, I'm not sure that I would have felt confident in going ahead with the film," he said in a piece for Focus Features. "Once I knew that she was on board—and had wanted me to direct—then I felt, 'We can do this.'" It came down to the admiration he had for Saoirse's craft and the way they could evolve the character together. "Because my safety net was, you can just put the camera on Saoirse in close-up—what she's thinking—and that will see you through a scene . . . At sixteen, Saoirse now has even more of a handle on her craft than she did at twelve."

Saoirse's experience with Wright foreshadowed what she would uncover with Gerwig—that moviemaking is not simply a director telling an actor what to do, but a true collaborative process that is continually evolving. "We had a great relationship on *Atonement*. I mean I was younger. I was about twelve when I did that. But I don't think there was [a] difference this time because Joe never really treated me like I was a kid," she told *Blackfilm*. "And then when we did *Hanna* together and that relationship just developed even further. And I guess we've gotten closer; and it really felt like a collaboration on this film."

From the Page to the Screen

Years after her *Hanna* reunion with Wright, Saoirse renewed another connection from the *Atonement* era. She starred as Florence Ponting in *On Chesil Beach* (2017), adapted from the novel of the same title by Ian McEwan. *On Chesil Beach* follows a young couple in the 1950s who suffer a disastrous wedding night and its subsequent fallout. McEwan, the author of *Atonement*, had seen several of his books adapted by this time, but *On Chesil Beach* was the first film he also wrote the screenplay for—and he had one casting in mind. As the *Daily Mail* reported, "For [McEwan] there was only ever one person who could play the heroine." Speaking of Saoirse, McEwan said, "I only see her when I read any page of *On Chesil Beach*."

McEwan's praise for Saoirse's acting ability and now-legendary range was effusive. He explained to *Newsweek*: "Saoirse has gifts of immediate emotional insight that any novelist must envy. She can make herself the ordinary girl next door and then, by a shift of expression, a turn of the head, assume great and unusual beauty. But above all, it's her intelligence that I cherish." In addition to her skill and intelligence, McEwan highlighted another element of Saoirse's character that frequently emerges when she is spoken of by others: her down-to-earth nature, unchanged by the time and tides of Hollywood celebrity. "Burgeoning fame hasn't swamped her," he said. "She remains firmly herself, and it's a lovely self, in which the natural twelve-year-old child still retains a fun-loving role."

Saoirse was thrilled to dive into a McEwan-envisioned world again. "Ian is someone who writes women incredibly skillfully, with a well-rounded perspective," she told *Newsweek*, while suggesting that *On Chesil Beach* wouldn't be their last collaboration. "I'd like to play another one written by him every ten years."

Billy Howle and Saoirse on set of *On Chesil Beach*, October 2016.

Saoirse and cast in *Mary Queen of Scots,* 2018.

Following: James McArdle and Saoirse attend the press night performance of *The Tragedy of Macbeth* at the Almeida Theatre, October 2021.

FRIENDS ON-SCREEN AND OFF

In addition to the "round robin" of directors and literary figures who adore her, and her ongoing association with Chalamet, Saoirse enjoys collaborating with friends who are also fellow actors. Often, they meet on one set and become so close that they are eager to work together again, pulling each other in when future projects arise. Saoirse's best friend is the actor Eileen O'Higgins, who was born in Northern Ireland. Theirs is a case of art mirroring life. O'Higgins played Nancy, the hometown best friend of Saoirse's character, Eilis, in *Brooklyn,* and the two have been inseparable ever since.

"That's the thing with this job: The people you get to meet. You get friends for life," O'Higgins told *Irish Life.* "Sometimes you cross paths with people and I do think you were meant to meet them. They just stay." The two soon reunited on-screen for *Mary Queen of Scots,* where O'Higgins played one of Mary's devoted ladies-in-waiting.

They are so close that O'Higgins was even Saoirse's date at the BAFTAs and then the Golden Globe Awards in 2018—which meant she got to witness her friend win Best Actress for *Lady Bird* and received a shout-out in her speech. "It was brilliant," O'Higgins told *Sunday World* of being in the room when Saoirse won. "It was really lovely to see one's friend achieving something so well deserved, and I've been very lucky to work with her twice. To be honest, the two of us are such good friends, that is who you'd nearly expect sitting next to you." When asked by *The Irish Sun* if she and Saoirse were in touch during the pandemic lockdown, O'Higgins answered, "Of course, she's like my right arm."

Another friend and frequent collaborator is the Scottish actor James McArdle. The McArdle connection stems from *Mary Queen of Scots*—he played Mary's half brother James, Earl of Moray. In the movie, they have a complicated relationship: Mary's return to Scotland takes power away from James, and he plots to dethrone and betray her. Yet a measure of affection remains between the siblings (despite all the scheming). Away from their characters, McArdle became a trusted friend of Saoirse's, with both actors thinking of each other for future projects. "Something felt right every time we worked together, which is quite rare," McArdle told the BBC.

As *British Vogue* wrote: "So, when Kate Winslet personally tapped Ronan to 'be her lover' in Francis Lee's *Ammonite* (2021), a period drama set on the Jurassic Coast in the 1840s, Ronan called McArdle to tell him about the role of her character's frigid Victorian husband, only to find out he'd already auditioned and landed the part." Then, when McArdle, a seasoned stage actor, was approached about a theatrical production of *Macbeth*, he knew at once who he would want opposite him.

He quipped to the magazine, "I got down on one knee and asked her to be my Lady Macbeth in the most romantic spot in Scotland: Leith." Their subsequent take on *The Tragedy of Macbeth*, which became one of the hottest tickets on London's West End, put a new focus on the main couple's romantic relationship and added freshly modern spice to one of the most well-known plays in the English language.

Any of the **actors** that I've **gotten on with** the **best** are the ones that I'll have a similar **sense of humor** with and you can just sort of **mess about** with them."

Jo March in *Little Women*

The version of Josephine "Jo" March that emerged from Saoirse and Gerwig's collaboration is distinct. She still has all the hallmarks that make Jo one of the most beloved characters in American literature—dogged independence, deep commitment to her life as a writer, and unwavering love for her family and friends. But what makes Jo such a timeless standout as a character is her resistance to the conventional roles women in her era were expected to play. Both Saoirse and Gerwig leaned in on this element and took their Jo even further.

Not only is Jo's neatly romantic ending with Professor Bhaer not given the fairytale wedding treatment here, but Gerwig gives Jo entirely new scenes that showcase a female artist coming into her own. As *Variety* wrote, "At the end of the new film, Gerwig invents a twist that Ronan executes to a T—a tribute to Alcott's trailblazing spirit in which [Jo] clashes with a stuffy and chauvinistic editor over the publication of her book. As Jo, Ronan demands concessions and refuses to back down." Rather than wrap Jo up with a glib married bow, as we usually leave her at the end of *Little Women*, the 2019 film shifts the narrative and puts the focus "not on love and marriage but on a woman who demands power in both art and commerce." Jo also has the chance to see the "birth" of her story into a novel on the printing press—a scene presented with joy and accomplishment after a long struggle to get it written and accepted for publication.

Gerwig was inspired to give Jo a new kind of conclusion after her extensive research into Louisa May Alcott's life. Unlike the heroine of her beloved fictional creation, "Louisa never got married, never had children, and kept the damn copyrights! She made so much money because of it. She supported her entire family, who had always been wretchedly poor. I just kept feeling—this is the thing underneath that all women have been unconsciously responding to."

Jo's more modern representation was more than just a twist—for Gerwig, it felt like a vital statement to make. Not just for Alcott, but for the progress of women since. She told *Variety*, "I felt if I could give Louisa an ending she actually wanted for Jo 150 years later, then maybe we've gotten somewhere."

Saoirse as Jo March in *Little Women*, 2019.

The WALTER KERR Theatre
ARTHUR MILLER'S
The CRUCIBLE.
The KERR
THRILLING AND MONUMENTAL
THE WALTER KERR THEATRE
8H55

chapter 6

From the Screen to the Stage

"It's been a real learning curve for me in just how much you can test yourself. Because you do feel that on film as well, but I think this is intensified. Every day, every hour is completely different. You could feel really confident for a while in what you are doing and feel really great going forward and then something happens that will knock you again."

—Saoirse Ronan on playing Lady Macbeth, the BBC

At age twenty-one, Saoirse had two Academy Award nominations and more than fifteen major film roles to her name. She was among the youngest in cinematic history to have claimed two nominations—an exclusive club that included Jennifer Lawrence and Angela Lansbury. With her Hollywood star burnished and gleaming, she turned to a new challenge, one that had served as a proving ground for actors for centuries.

The sign outside The Walter Kerr Theatre of *The Crucible* starring Saoirse, April 2016.

It was a pursuit she'd considered part of her story since her father, Paul, first made the leap from bartending to New York City's theatrical scene. As a babe in arms at her father's rehearsals, stage performance was Saoirse's first exposure to the world of acting that she would come to make her own. For this reason, she waited until she felt she was truly ready before making the leap herself.

"I had always said I wouldn't do a play until I was in my early twenties," Saoirse related in a 2016 interview with *IrishCentral*. "My father started in theater and so I was aware of the discipline and commitment it took to put on a show, so I felt that by the time I reached the age of twenty-one, twenty-two, I'd have been acting for over ten years and that would be the right time to try it."

The timing seemed to align perfectly in the wake of *Brooklyn*'s success, as Saoirse was offered a starring role in one of the most famous—and famously challenging—plays of the twentieth century, Arthur Miller's *The Crucible*.

THE GIRL WHO CRIED WITCH

Working on *The Crucible* was not only a watershed moment for Saoirse's career—it was also an important time that allowed her to reconnect with New York City.

"New York was always where I wanted to go, but I wasn't ready when I was nineteen," she told *Time Out*. She went on, explaining how the move to the city also aligned with her desire to live as normal a life as she could. "I never wanted to just be, you know, a child actor who grew up in this unrealistic world where, okay, you're working hard, but everything's done for you. I wanted to have a real experience of someone who hates fucking paying their bills and washing their clothes, but you just have to do it because that's what you do. It's lovely to be able to walk out on the street or go to a bar and be sitting next to, you know, a taxi driver or a lawyer."

The theatre marquee unveiling of *The Crucible* at The Walter Kerr Theatre, February 2016.

Following: Saoirse attends the 70th Annual Tony Awards, June 2016.

"I wanted to have a real experience of someone who hates fucking paying their bills and washing their clothes, but you just have to do it because that's what you do."

My father started in theater and so I was aware of the discipline and commitment it took to put on a show.

While in her free time Saoirse was able to have that normal life, her new play kept her busy. She took on the role of Abigail Williams, a young Puritan woman who is considered the story's antagonist. Abigail is the ringleader of the girls in Salem, Massachusetts, who fall into witchcraft hysteria and end up falsely accusing dozens of their neighbors of consorting with the devil. Throughout the course of the play, Abigail moves from her powerless position as a disgraced servant to become one of the most powerful and feared figures in Salem. *Variety* says that Abigail, "like an unethical politician . . . manipulates her pliable band of orphaned servant girls into a rapturous, unthinking mob." It's a notoriously difficult part, responsible for driving the narrative's momentum and providing its tension.

"Abigail is a doozy of a role to pick as your Broadway debut," *Time Out*'s Joshua Rothkopf pointed out in an interview. Saoirse answered with her trademark frankness: "I'm realizing that more and more every day. We've only had the first week of rehearsals. This isn't just my Broadway debut: I've never done stage before. It's very scary, but I'm very lucky."

There was another factor that initially drew Saoirse to the role of Abigail. When she first read the play, she saw something in the character that she recognized. "Abigail reminded me of a character I played years ago in *Atonement*," she told *BroadwayWorld*. "I like the fact that she's got this strong spirit and will do whatever she has to do to achieve her goal. She's the antagonist, but with so many layers to explore."

Just as she felt defensive of Briony, Saoirse wanted to better understand a pivotal female character who is the recipient of the audience's scorn. She took the time to investigate Abigail's motivations, read about the history of the seventeenth century culture Abigail was raised in, and eschewed the generally accepted idea of her as *The Crucible*'s villain. On *Good Morning America*, Saoirse said that Abigail is "the worst" but then was quick to add: "She's got her reasons to be the worst. I don't think it would be fair to say that she's just a sort of simple black-and-white villain. I think usually the best sort of antagonists aren't."

"She's got her reasons to be the worst. I don't think it would be fair to say that she's just a sort of simple black-and-white villain. I think usually the best sort of antagonists aren't."

The 2016 *Crucible* revival was directed and given new life by "high-concept theater heavyweight" and Belgian theater director, Ivo van Hove. *The New York Times* declared in its review that "an endlessly revived historical drama from 1953 suddenly feels like the freshest, scariest play in town." Saoirse shared top billing with Ben Whishaw (of *Skyfall*) as the object of her obsession and revenge, John Proctor; Sophie Okonedo (of *Hotel Rwanda*) as his unjustly targeted wife, Elizabeth; and Ciarán Hinds (of *Belfast*) as the hanging judge, Deputy Governor Danforth. *Variety* called their ensemble acting "superb," while *The Times* went with "dazzling."

Saoirse won critical plaudits for her Broadway debut, proving that she was more than capable of transmuting her on-screen alchemy into an environment with a live audience. *The Times* hailed her "changeling beauty" and said, "she's absolutely smashing in the part," concluding that "*The Crucible* has a diverse and spectacular assortment of moments that make the flesh creep. But there's nothing quite as scary as the sight of Ms. Ronan's Abigail, seated stock-still in a chair, bending a vulnerable girl to her will with the force of a malevolent stare."

RENEWING A SHAKESPEAREAN TRAGEDY

The Crucible introduced Saoirse to the rigors and rewards of theatrical productions. She was clearly as gifted onstage as on-screen, but the next few years would prove to be so packed with movies that she wouldn't appear in another play until 2022. There she embodied one of the most iconic female roles ever scripted—Lady Macbeth, in a reshaped interpretation of Shakespeare's work, mounted under its full title *The Tragedy of Macbeth*.

The performance—her first Shakespearean undertaking—meant another debut for Saoirse, this time on London's West End. She was reunited with actor and close friend James McArdle, who had played her scheming brother in *Mary Queen of Scots*. Together they would bring to the stage "a fresh take" (*The Hollywood Reporter*) on a play estimated to have been first performed in 1606.

In *The Tragedy of Macbeth*, the ruthless Lady Macbeth works to persuade her husband to kill King Duncan, who is their guest. After the crime is committed and the couple ascends to the throne of Scotland, Macbeth becomes increasingly tyrannical, and his wife is plagued by guilt and remorse. She slowly goes mad under the strain, until she is sleepwalking through the castle, desperate to wash imagined bloodstains from her hands, during which she delivers the famous line, "Out, damned spot! Out, I say!"

Saoirse's turn as Lady Macbeth, directed by Yaël Farber at the Almeida Theatre, marked a time of renewal for a theater-loving city that saw its house lights go dark for more than a year. The long-simmering production had been delayed by the global pandemic. *Vogue* wrote in a profile of Saoirse and McArdle that their *Macbeth* was "the hottest ticket in an autumn season [and] billed as the rebirth of London theatre."

Saoirse attends the press night performance of *The Tragedy of Macbeth* at The Almeida Theatre, London, October 2021.

The Mare of Easttown Comes to Macbeth

Both stars of *Macbeth*, Saoirse and James McArdle, have worked closely with Kate Winslet. McArdle appeared with Winslet in the acclaimed TV drama *Mare of Easttown*, about a downtrodden detective investigating a horrific murder in a small Pennsylvania town, and in the Francis Lee-directed period piece *Ammonite* (2020). Saoirse also starred in *Ammonite*, playing the lover of Winslet's character, paleontologist Mary Anning.

Winslet and Saoirse shared scenes of intimacy with Winslet stepping in to use her more extensive cinematic background to ground their romantic coupling. When it came time to shoot their love scene, Winslet had the matter in hand. "I've definitely had more experience and played LGBTQ characters in the past," Winslet told *Variety*. "It just made sense. Women know what women want, let's not beat about the bush. Saoirse and I knew we could unite in our feelings about these characters and where they're at, and to tell that story physically. It was a very joyful experience."

When the *Macbeth* pair were interviewed for *British Vogue*, they reported that Winslet was coming out to see them take the stage. They also offered some intriguing insight into one of the world's most renowned actors.

"She sends voice memos that are obscene," said McArdle. "And I love every one of them." Saoirse confirmed: "She's got a potty mouth."

Kate Winslet and Saoirse in *Ammonite*, 2020.

Saoirse told the magazine that she was moved by the long lines of people eager for the chance to support in-person arts again. "When the theatre is finally at capacity, there will be so much goodwill in the audience," she said. "It will hardly even matter if a play is bad." *Vogue* continued: "There's little chance of that with *Macbeth* . . . And, as is so often the case with Shakespeare, *Macbeth* feels almost terrifyingly pertinent to the current moment: a society populated by individuals who cannot distinguish between reality and fantasy; tyrannical leaders blinded by ambition; a natural world distinctly out of sorts . . . In lieu of traditional sets and costumes, the Almeida's staging will feel apocalyptic and outside time."

The London production made the couple's relationship its centerpiece. "In every production we've seen, it's the dynamic between the Macbeths that fascinates us," McArdle told *Vogue*. "The play is about the tragedy of the Macbeths, not Macbeth alone." Saoirse agreed: "You're rooting for them . . . They're both kind of terrible, but you're fascinated by their incredibly modern, liberated relationship."

Saoirse related to *Vogue* that despite having Broadway's Abigail Williams under her belt, she was "absolutely terrified" to undertake *Macbeth*. "I do feel unbelievably nervous," she told the BBC. "You get

"You get hit with waves of panic and terror, and I'm not kidding about that. You do feel suddenly stuck for a minute in anxiety about what you're doing. But then you pull yourself out of it."

hit with waves of panic and terror, and I'm not kidding about that. You do feel suddenly stuck for a minute in anxiety about what you're doing. But then you pull yourself out of it."

She needn't have worried. *The Hollywood Reporter* said of the leads: "together they're sensational, in what feels like a generational-best *Macbeth*, while Saoirse herself was "an alluring, icily enigmatic presence." *London Theatre*'s review headline stated that "Saoirse Ronan stuns," and of her performance that, "Ronan's delivery makes you lean in and listen, lending her all the more control of the action. She doesn't need to shout to make her Lady Macbeth powerful; all she needs is you to watch her, which you can't help doing." *Independent* observed, "It's a rare skill to make Shakespeare's beautiful but weighty words easy to understand, but Ronan manages it. Speaking with her own Irish accent, she adds modern inflections to famous lines and breathes new life into them."

Writing for *The Standard*, critic Nick Curtis noted, "I can't remember a debut as hotly anticipated as Saoirse Ronan's. The luminous, four-time Oscar-nominee doesn't disappoint." Curtis went on, "Thanks to a subtle edit of the text, this is very much a tragedy that happens to a couple, rather than just to James McArdle's meaty, tormented Macbeth. There's a pristine clarity to the two leads' performances and to Farber's direction." *Express* waxed rhapsodic about Saoirse, saying that she is "[a]s mesmerizing on stage as she is on film," and they add a description that feels fitting for Saoirse: "Although it is hard to take your eyes off her, she is also a true company player, shining but never outshining, never pulling focus in this triumphant ensemble piece."

Though Saoirse hasn't taken another stage role since making two of the most renowned roles uniquely her own, she's all but certain to tread the boards again.

Lady Macbeth in *The Tragedy of Macbeth*

How do you take one of the most well-known characters in literature and one of the most resonant roles in the history of theater and make them your own? First you make her even more present: Saoirse's Lady Macbeth is given additional stage time in Farber's "refreshed" *The Tragedy of Macbeth*, involved in scenes and activities where prior stagings since the 1600s had her waiting in the wings.

Second, you make her stand out: Saoirse used her Irish accent in the role, the sole actor with that inflection. And third, you reframe the narrative: The couple's relationship was central to the play's storyline, snatching the attention from witches, regicide, bloody ghosts, and moving forests.

Saoirse and costar James McArdle also reenvisioned their characters as they zoomed in on what they viewed as a tragic love story. Thinking about them in modern terms rather than seeking inspiration from past productions or Shakespearean traditions, they even gave them private, everyday names—Susan and Neil Macbeth—"because this is a domestic tragedy about a couple." Saoirse explained to BBC News that they thought of their characters as engaged in a "Kim [Kardashian] and Kanye [West] situation," drawing inspiration from the idea of "a modern power couple that is professional but also has tenderness . . . [with] so much of their private life that we don't know."

Although Shakespeare's timeless script was not altered, this *Macbeth* gave lines and presence to Lady Macbeth that involved her further in the action and also made sense in terms of her character's ultimate unraveling. In his review for *The Hollywood Reporter*, Demetrios Matheou sets the scene: "Not only is Lady Macbeth given the messenger's lines warning Lady Macduff of the approaching assassins, but she is in the room to witness the slaughter, which is brutally, shockingly executed. The queen's horrified response is so astonishingly well-conveyed by Ronan that it's conceivable the undoing Lady Macbeth subsequently succumbs to is a form of PTSD. This scene alone is stunning, superb theater."

chapter 7

Redirecting the Spotlight

"There was me at twenty-seven thinking about stopping because I felt self-conscious or like I didn't know how to do it. And then watching this twenty-three-year-old carry the weight of a huge film like that with ease and grace and majesty. It was remarkable to watch. She makes it look so easy, like breathing. It was totally inspiring."

—Jack Lowden on Saoirse's performance as Mary Stuart

From breakout child star to top-billed leading lady, Saoirse has still managed to keep the spotlight off her personal life. Not only is that a feat considering the public's voracious appetite for celebrity news, but it points to her own savvy and expertise in handling her image. It's also the payoff of her long-stated desire to lead as balanced a lifestyle as possible, even though the movie-star milieu she grew up in invited everything but balance.

Saoirse attends the 3rd Annual Academy Museum Gala, December 2023.

Following: Saoirse posing at CinemaCon in Nevada, April 2018.

"If you don't have your mam telling you, 'Remember, you're still my daughter,' you're going to go off the rails."

"I want to naturally be able to grow up as a normal person," she told *Time Out London* in 2013. At nineteen, she was fully aware of how much could have gone awry, and how much of her successful path she's owed to her family's grounding influence, especially that of her mother, Monica. "If you don't have your mam telling you, 'Remember, you're still my daughter,' you're going to go off the rails."

By all known accounts, Saoirse has remained on the rails. There are no sordid tattler stories about her off-hours exploits; no intrusive paparazzi shots sold to the highest bidder. She has done reams of publicity, charming interviewers with her frankness and good humor. But she almost always keeps the conversation focused on her work and the people involved in that work. When she does venture into more personal territory, it's frequently in service of an opinion for social good—her advocacy for women, children, the LGBTQ+ community, or the environment. She remains active in charity work, especially in Ireland, where her involvement in local campaigns can cause a stir.

She is a long-term ambassador for the Irish Society for the Prevention of Cruelty to Children (ISPCC) and its Childline service, which provides a phone number that children can call to report situations of abuse. In addition to her involvement with ISPCC, Saoirse has been outspoken about issues of equality, especially in regard to gender, reproductive rights, and sexual orientation. When asked about her 2015 vote in favor of Ireland's Same-Sex Marriage referendum and speaking at a campaign event organized by the Yes Equality group, Saoirse told *Pride Source*, "So many of my friends are gay. And especially in the arts, I'm surrounded by people of all different sexual orientations all the time. The best thing about the experience of being in this world is that everyone just becomes this one thing and, for me anyway, there's never been any sort of separation at all or segregation." When the marriage referendum won, as *The Gentlewoman* reported, Saoirse, who was still posting then on Twitter (now known as X), wrote exuberantly: "I LOVE YOU IRELAND!!!!! IT'S A BEAUTIFUL DAY!"

"The best thing about the experience of being in this world is that everyone just becomes this one thing and, for me anyway, there's never been any sort of separation at all or segregation."

Saoirse attends the Gucci Cruise show in France, May 2018.

In 2016, she backed the activists behind Home Sweet Home, a campaign against homelessness in Ireland, when they took over an empty office block in Dublin in an effort to house the city's homeless. Joining her were other well-known Irish creatives like musicians Hozier and Glen Hansard, and playwright/director Jim Sheridan, whose 1989 movie, *My Left Foot,* received worldwide acclaim and reinvigorated the Irish film industry.

She also threw her public support behind the referendum vote to repeal Ireland's abortion ban. In a 2018 *Vogue* profile—written by Irish novelist Sally Rooney, now a global superstar in her own right—Rooney asked if Saoirse was afraid of backlash for her stance on a politically fraught topic. Saoirse was adamant in her response.

"I just felt like that wasn't important," she said of any potential blowback. "I know people who had to travel abroad in order to get an abortion, and that's when I knew I would speak out." Weeks later, after the referendum received a landslide vote in favor of repealing the abortion ban, Saoirse was described as feeling elated and "so proud" about the vote's results, "to see family and friends, and people I wouldn't have expected to vote yes, choose to give Irishwomen their rights."

Saoirse has said that she doesn't consider herself to be an activist, because she thinks it would be unfair to claim that title in comparison to people who dedicate their lives to vital causes. Instead, she uses the influence her fame brings to try and call attention and broader support to issues she is passionate about, per *The Hollywood Reporter*. "Being a mouthpiece for the people that actually know what they're talking about is really how I always felt about it," she said in 2020.

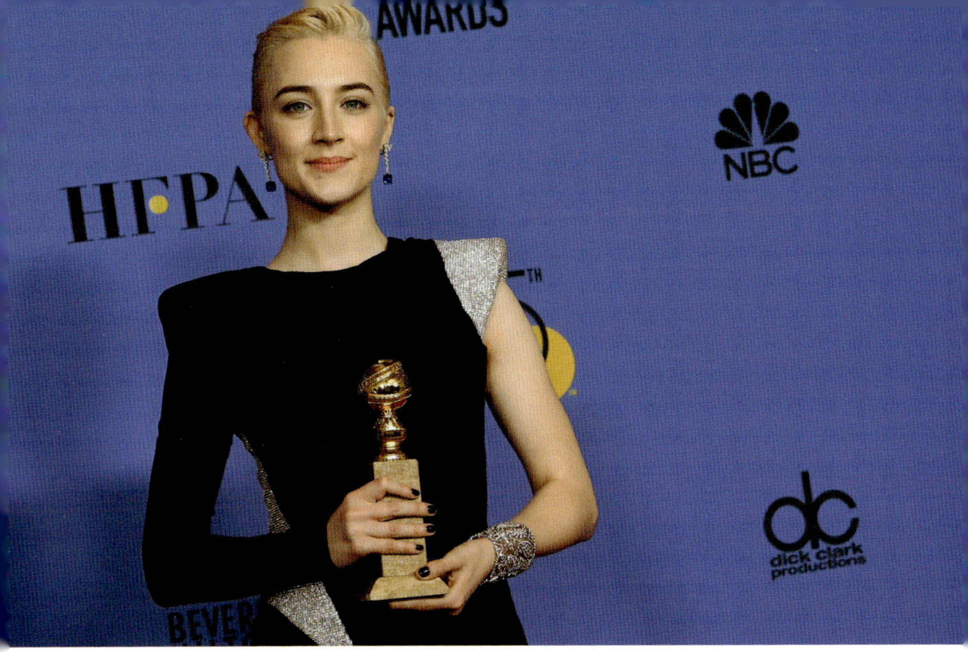

Saoirse poses with the award for Best Performance by an Actress in a Motion Picture Musical or Comedy for *Lady Bird* at the 75th Annual Golden Globe Awards, January 2018.

FASHION SPEAKS

Saoirse has also used another medium where she receives attention—fashion—to spread messages about causes she believes in. As a movie star, she makes frequent appearances in fabulous outfits, and she is considered a fashion icon in her own right. In recent years, she's also aimed to make an impact spearheading sustainable fashion and eco-conscious designers. *Two Thirds* describes her as "one of the leading lights of Hollywood's newfound drive to champion eco-fashion causes and sustainable fashion labels." Photographs of her red-carpet looks travel far and wide, and can receive detailed coverage—so why not make a statement with what she's wearing?

As her involvement in disparate spheres has shown, Saoirse's impact on popular culture reaches far beyond cinematic lines. She regularly uses her voice and platform to lobby for social good, and even her red-carpet outfits can speak volumes. In 2018, she went to collect

her Best Actress Golden Globe for *Lady Bird* in a stunning black and silver Versace dress. The dress sported broad shoulders, and kept one arm covered and the other sleeveless, while a bold openwork diamond bracelet from Cartier circled her wrist like a gauntlet. Though she looked as chic and elegant as ever, there was far more to her Globes style than met the eye. The awards ceremony was taking place amid Hollywood's Time's Up movement, which was prompting women to speak out against abusive figures in power and combat endemic sexual harassment in the workplace.

Saoirse and her team did their part to ensure that her dress and preparations that evening reflected the moment, even recommissioning and reimagining the dress to turn it black, the color of solidarity with Time's Up. Her stylist Elizabeth Saltzman told *British Vogue* that they worked directly with Donatella and Allegra Versace to rework the dress, and that the resulting design "[is] not about sex, it's about strength. It's not about frivolity, it's about confidence, excellence, purity, and support."

But Saoirse's commitment to backing Time's Up went beyond a singular evening or outfit. Saltzman explained, "Saoirse and I had a conversation at the beginning of the season that should *Lady Bird* go the distance, we wanted to work with all females—female make-up [artists], female hairstylists, female designers—and that we would never talk about it to anyone. It would be our fun secret, our empowering moment." How like Saoirse to make a vital statement, and to empower fellow women, without seeing a need to declare what she had done in advance for credit.

She made another outfit impact at the 2020 Oscars, where all eyes were on her as a Best Actress nominee for *Little Women*. She stepped onto the red carpet wearing a gorgeous black Gucci halter dress with a deep-cut neckline and a skirt of satin moire in an eye-catching lilac shade. But she wasn't just wearing Gucci—the dress was upcycled

---

Saoirse walking the red carpet at the 90th Annual Academy Awards, March 2018.

with surplus fabric from another dress she'd worn to the recent BAFTA Awards. *ELLE UK* wrote that Saoirse—"with help from her stylist Elizabeth Saltzman and Gucci Creative Director Alessandro Michele"—was among the celebrities who "used the glamorous affair to perfectly illustrate how new needn't cost the earth." Climate activist Venetia La Manna told *ELLE UK*: "This is absolutely an important and meaningful change" because "these celebrities have such huge platforms, it would be brilliant to see them strive to re-wear and upcycle past red carpet looks time and time again—not just for awards season, but for TV and promotional appearances too." And Saoirse has continued to do just that.

> "Saoirse and I had a conversation at the beginning of the season that should *Lady Bird* go the distance, we wanted to work with all females . . . It would be our fun secret, our empowering moment."

—Elizabeth Saltzman on Saoirse, 2018

Forty Million Views and Counting

Saoirse has used her celebrity to promote causes she believes in and boost awareness in other areas of pop culture. In 2016, she was featured in the music video for Hozier's song "Cherry Wine." The song addresses domestic violence, and in the video, Saoirse appears as a woman who seems to be in an idyllic relationship. Yet intercut between scenes of playful domesticity, she stands before a mirror gazing at her reflection and slowly removes her makeup to reveal a black eye.

The contrast of the song, which seems on its surface sweet and gentle but whose lyrics explore abusive episodes, is further mirrored in the video's narrative. "I like that the video doesn't show the actual abuse, it chooses to show us their loving moments and then her black eye when she's alone," reads one of the most upvoted comments on the video. "Frequently that's how it works." Another notes, "I love how Saoirse's acting can pull us in with just her face. She doesn't even have to say anything." To date, the video has received more than forty million views on YouTube.

Hozier called "Cherry Wine" "a love song about the awful parts of love," and he used its release as a single to generate awareness for the campaign #FaceUpToDomesticViolence, with proceeds going to support anti-domestic violence charities. Saoirse joined him in promoting the campaign, releasing a statement that read, "I am equally honoured to join Hozier to create awareness for the #FaceUpToDomesticViolence campaign with the release of 'Cherry Wine' as a charity single . . . I hope through the video and song we can shine light on the issue and complexity of domestic abuse and in doing so help those caught up in the cycle of domestic violence."

Jack Lowden and Saoirse in *Mary Queen of Scots*, 2018.

Opposite: Jack Lowden and Saoirse attend the 27th British Independent Film Awards, December 2024.

A LOW-KEY LOVE STORY

Saoirse's career has included shining moments in the spotlight and fearlessly supporting global movements for good. From the outside, she seemed to have succeeded in her long-stated desire to grow up into a "regular person," and an exemplary one at that. But owing to her closely guarded private life, fans were left wondering about romance. After falling in love—or running from it—countless times on screen, had she ever discovered someone for her in the real world?

In the midst of making acclaimed movies and landing roles of a lifetime, Saoirse appears to have found a supportive and dynamic match in a fellow actor who understands her experiences and shares her desire to be involved in other sides of the storytelling process.

Jack Lowden was her first publicly confirmed relationship. While rumors in the past linked Saoirse to possible romantic interests, she stuck to her script of keeping her private life private and was never a plus-one at award shows until Lowden. Whenever she brought a "date" to an event, it was often a close friend or family. Saoirse and Lowden's relationship was kept strictly out of frame for a long while, developing what *US Weekly* terms a "low-key" timeline. "Low-key" is the go-to term that the media often uses when describing the pair.

Buzz and speculation that Saoirse and Lowden were dating went back as far as 2018 and their film, *Mary Queen of Scots,* where Lowden played Mary's first husband, Lord Darnley. Charming at first as he wins his queen, Darnley is revealed to be debauched and often inebriated, too easily tempted into treachery and betrayal. The handsome, affable Lowden seemed to have all of Darnley's charm without the treachery. On set and off, the two grew close, and the chattering classes took notice.

Both stayed mum on the subject. Lowden also seemed to share Saoirse's desire for privacy. "Oh, I'm not going to talk about that. I don't like talking about that side of life," he said in a 2019 interview with *ES Magazine,* when questions turned to their word-on-the-street romance. "Most of the actors I know live pretty normal lives, it's just every now and again they have to do something ridiculous or extraordinary. My life hasn't changed. People seem more interested—I guess that's changed, for sure."

Their relationship came to be public knowledge through small hints and a lot of sleuthing from those who were invested in the (alleged) love story. Unlike Saoirse, who has no presence on social media, Lowden is active on Instagram. So when images from their increasingly entwined worlds surfaced, they became further fuel for fans and the press. Saoirse sometimes showed up in a picture Lowden posted and later deleted; particularly ardent internet detectives pointed out when she was present, even just the back of her head.

In 2023, rumors that they were engaged were also sparked by a Lowden Instagram gallery. He uploaded several pictures from a hike through the gorgeous Scottish countryside in Perthshire with the caption, "the heather starting to put her purple on." In one picture, four hands (and, adorably, a dog paw) can be seen grouped together. Eagle-eyed fans thought they recognized Saoirse's hand—which was wearing a ring. When Saoirse and Lowden married in 2024, it was kept firmly under wraps. Coverage of the event only broke after the fact, with the marriage taking place in "a secret ceremony" in Edinburgh, Scotland, according to the *Irish Independent*. It was reported that "[o]nly a handful of the couple's closest friends were present—and all the guests were sworn to secrecy."

While they never confirmed their engagement by way of any spokespeople, they "refused to deny that Lowden proposed," as the *Irish Independent* put it. Saoirse began making more frequent appearances on his Instagram, including intimate snaps with the two appearing

Saoirse and Jack Lowden at the Australian Open at Melbourne Park, January 2022.

in a mirror selfie and embracing at the Glastonbury Festival. She was finally letting some of her private moments go beyond her inner circle, reflecting how close and confident she and Lowden were as a couple.

When it comes to questions about yet another potential stage of evolution for the Ronan-Lowdens, Saoirse has been candid. In a 2024 interview with *British Vogue*, writer Reni Edoo-Lodge and Saoirse spoke frankly about the expectations they felt from others around family life, as well as their own aspirations. When asked whether she wanted to have children, Saoirse answered, "Yes, I do." She went on, "I became successful when I was quite young. So it meant that, actually, by the time I found my partner, I'm not at the stage where if it happened, I would like to have a kid. I feel fortunate enough that if I step out of this for a minute, I'm hopefully not giving it up forever. But, yeah, I've always wanted that."

"I would like to have a kid. I feel fortunate enough that if I step out of this for a minute, I'm hopefully not giving it up forever. But, yeah, I've always wanted that."

Saoirse attends the Louis Vuitton Cruise 2026 show at Palais des Papes, France, May 2025.

Saoirse in *The Outrun*, 2024.

Following: Saoirse and Jack Lowden attend the 78th British Academy Film Awards at The Royal Festival Hall, February 2025.

THE FAMILY BUSINESS

Now that the world knows they're married, and unwanted speculation has become a thing of the past, Saoirse and Lowden are more open about discussing their partnership. It's a union that expanded beyond domestic life and into their professional fields as well, as both are interested in producing films.

Lowden has worked as a producer previously, with a particular interest in centering stories and productions in Scotland. Born in England but raised in the small Scottish Borders town of Oxton, Lowden's "unwavering loyalty" to Scotland, as *The Standard* put it, comes through in interviews and profiles. "It's a place I'm enormously proud of," he told *The Standard* in 2019. This is reflected in his commitment to Scottish-made productions, which he's been involved in behind the scenes for years. "I want to shoot more stuff there and have more of a hand in it," he explained. "I want to make as much work in Scotland as possible."

In 2024, Saoirse and Lowden coproduced their first film together in Scotland, *The Outrun*. Lowden's star is also on the rise, keeping him busy on multiple fronts. Like Saoirse, Lowden has been acting since he was a child, working with the Scottish Youth Theatre and attending the Royal Conservatoire of Scotland.

Originally trained as a stage actor, he had breakout roles on television in the BBC's *War & Peace* miniseries and in movies like director Christopher Nolan's *Dunkirk* prior to *Mary Queen of Scots*. Since 2022, he's made waves as disgraced MI5 agent River Cartwright in Apple TV+'s exceptional spy drama *Slow Horses*, starring opposite Gary Oldman. In 2024, he was nominated for an Emmy for Outstanding Supporting Actor in a Drama Series for *Slow Horses*. Saoirse attended the ceremony with him, making the occasion their red-carpet debut as a married couple.

Lowden was also announced to play Mr. Darcy in a Netflix TV series adaptation of Jane Austen's classic *Pride and Prejudice*. Considering the longstanding affection that audiences have for *Pride and Prejudice* and Netflix's success with period romance adaptations, that role is sure to launch Lowden to even greater heights. According to Saoirse, though, her husband is practical and pragmatic, and he's sure to take his spiking levels of fame in stride.

"Jack is a lot calmer than I am," Saoirse said in a 2024 interview with *USA Today*, recounting her time making Steve McQueen's *Blitz* and working with Lowden on *The Outrun*. It's a rare glimpse into the private side of their dynamic, both personally and professionally. "He's my voice of reason. But as a duo, we've both been on film sets our whole lives, so we have an appreciation of what we're asking actors to do. We always want them to feel safe."

EE
BAFTA
FILM AWARDS

"Jack is a lot calmer than I am . . . He's my voice of reason."

Saoirse in a scene in *The Outrun*, 2024.

With the relationship cat out of the bag, Lowden is not shy about expressing appreciation for his wife and singing paeans to her talent. "My first love is actors, and when you're given a Ferrari like her, it's all about how you make everything good for the Ferrari to show off," he said, when speaking about Saoirse's performance in *The Outrun*. "Don't make a Ferrari do what a Renault Clio does. It's a dreadful analogy, but they're like gold dust, good actors."

Not only did Saoirse star as *The Outrun*'s protagonist, Rona, but she also coproduced it with Lowden. According to the *LA Times,* Lowden handed her a copy of Amy Liptrot's addiction memoir of the same name, saying, "This is what you should do next." Saoirse also worked closely with German director Nora Fingscheidt (*System Crasher*) and Liptrot in the adaptation process.

Circumstances around the film also meant that Saoirse created a lot of her own dialogue. As the *LA Times* reported, "Because English is a

Saoirse as Rona in *The Outun*, 2024.

second language for Fingscheidt, she wrote the script loosely, without specific dialogue, leaving it up to the actors to know what to say."

"It was a bit unusual for me to work like that," Saoirse said. "But because I would love to make my own stuff, it gave me a bit more confidence to know that when it came to that stage of developing a film, I wasn't completely clueless. I could find a way to use my own voice and translate that into dialogue."

Saoirse was further drawn to the role for personal reasons—and feeling that she was in a stage of her life where she was ready to see them represented on-screen. In interviews for *The Outrun*, she has been forthright about watching people close to her struggle with addiction and alcoholism. Per *The Times*, it is "something that has played a huge part in my life, battling for the love and the attention of someone and them not being able to choose me over this substance." The subject is not one that is often explored with nuance in films, especially where women are concerned. Saoirse added, "And there's a uniqueness in watching a young woman on-screen struggle with alcohol addiction."

Lowden was behind her every step of the way, though he never doubted that Saoirse would be able to tackle the film's unique challenges. "She's not an overly precious actor," he explained to *Vogue*. "She's an actor who is built for projects that ask a lot of everybody involved, and *The Outrun* asked a lot of her." He added, "I've acted with her, and now I've produced with her, and there's never been a single moment where I felt like she was lost or didn't know what she needed to do," he says. "She's like a Swiss Army knife."

Saoirse and Jack also plan to maintain their working partnership, with Saoirse highlighting that they bring out the best in each other. "If you find people that you love and you trust creatively, why would you not want to keep working with them?" she pointed out to *The Sunday Times*.

As for whether the couple will star on-screen again together, that seems to be a hot topic of conversation in the Ronan-Lowden household. "Jack didn't want to for a long time, but I've now convinced him that's a great idea," Saoirse explained, regarding any plans for another double-billed film. But it may be that their next collaboration as costars could return them to a different medium. "I'd really like to do something together on stage."

"She's an actor who is built for projects that ask a lot of everybody involved, and *The Outrun* asked a lot of her."

—Jack Lowden on Saoirse, 2024

Saoirse and Jack Lowden attend the 76th Primetime Emmy Awards at Peacock Theater, September 2024.

abc
hulu

Rona in *The Outrun*

While an early decision made in the adaptation process was to change the main "character's" name, to give creative distance to both memoirist Amy Liptrot and the production side, it was Liptrot's distinctive narrative voice that pulled Saoirse in, because of "how she depicted an addiction story and how it was so much more than that." To prepare for the role of a young woman trying for sobriety after years of addiction, Saoirse visited Alcoholics Anonymous meetings—and in the film, when Rona is in similar support groups, the scenes include actual addicts in recovery.

"They've gone to the depths of their soul to get to where they are now, which produces an honesty and a sense of humor about it all," Saoirse explained to *Screen Daily*. "If I hadn't experienced that first-hand, it's not an aspect I would have incorporated into the character." She also spoke extensively with Liptrot about her life, as well as consulting with close friends. "I've watched people I love change because of addiction. There's a helplessness you feel when you watch someone you love—friends my age and one in particular who I'm close to—go through that."

The Outrun is told in non-linear form, meaning that viewers witness Rona in various stages of addiction and recovery throughout. This meant that Saoirse was called on to play a broad range of physical and emotional states, depicting both intoxication and withdrawal. To assist her in physically embodying these stages, she consulted with Sir Wayne McGregor, the resident choreographer of The Royal Ballet. "I wanted to make sure that each time we saw Rona under the influence, we weren't just repeating the same point again and again," she told *Vogue*. "There are points at which it's important to look at this character and see that she's having a great time—she's dancing and laughing and seems like someone you might love to hang out with for a night. But watching her reach a tipping point is what really grounds you in the reality of her illness."

Saoirse in *The Outrun*, 2024.

Conclusion

Taking the Reins

"Some directors make the mistake of thinking that one size fits all. And while, yes, you have to be a leader, actually for the best results, you have to bend towards your actors-adjust to them and make them feel they can do anything."

—Saoirse on directing

Beyond award shows and accolades, what does the future hold for Saoirse Ronan? What seems certain is that she is determined to carve her own path forward. Her slate of movies in 2024 were of a distinctly more mature and independent bent than those that came before. One such occurrence was director Steve McQueen's World War II film *Blitz*. When the opportunity to work with McQueen (*12 Years a Slave*) arose, Saoirse started working with a singing coach to prove that she was more than capable of carrying a tune and improving her vocal stylings.

Saoirse attends the 92nd Annual Academy Awards at Hollywood and Highland, February 2020.

“It was the first time in a long time I was properly pitching myself,” she relayed to *Screen Daily*, running through the list of what she assured McQueen she was capable of taking on. “‘I can do accents, sure I can sing, I can be a mother, I can do all these things,’ not knowing if I actually could.”

McQueen, impressed, offered her the role of young mother, Rita, who is separated from her child in wartime Britain. Rita has several scenes where she sings, and by the time filming commenced, Saoirse was more than up to the task. “She’s the real deal. She’s more than the real deal; she has a certain sensibility. She makes the ordinary look extraordinary,” the director told *Variety* of his experience working with Saoirse.

Rita was a new kind of role for Saoirse—her first as a mother, after so many years of playing daughters. But it was the unique historical angle of the film that also appealed to her. “To be able to show this

Saoirse and Elliott Heffernan in *Blitz*, 2024.

"She's the real deal. She's more than the real deal; she has a certain sensibility. She makes the ordinary look extraordinary."

—director Steve McQueen on Saoirse

Saoirse in an emotional scene in *Blitz*, 2024.

Elliott Heffernan and Saoirse in *Blitz*, 2024.

Following: Saoirse poses on the red carpet of the British Academy Film Awards in London, February 2025.

other side of what was happening in the war and how it affected mixed-race couples and mixed-race children—and children in general and women—was so fascinating," she told *LA Times*. Her own distinctly lived experiences influenced her on set with her young costar Elliott Heffernan, who played Rita's son, George, and was ten years old at the time of filming. "With Saoirse, she was not only protective of Elliott, but she understood him, because of course she started to act when she was nine herself," McQueen related to *New York Times*.

If *Blitz* was a stepping stone into more mature work, *The Outrun,* which also came out in 2024, was another significant progression for Saoirse's career. For the first time she officially took on multiple roles in the production. And she's clearly caught the bug ever since. Saoirse already has a new project as a producer lined up: director Sean Durkin's *Deep Cuts*. The movie's logline reads, "Two music-loving twentysomethings face love, ambition, and growing up during the 2000s, a decade that changed everything." Saoirse is also set to star in the movie alongside Austin Butler.

Saoirse has been increasingly vocal about her desire to direct. What began as casual commentary back in the *Lady Bird* and *Little Women* days with Greta Gerwig has now become a main talking point. "I'd love to do that [directing] next. That was always a passion of mine," she told *The Hollywood Reporter* at *The Outrun*'s LA premiere.

In a *Vanity Fair* interview at the Telluride Film Festival, where *The Outrun* was screening and Saoirse was also given the Silver Medallion Award for recognition of achievements in the film industry, Saoirse reiterated that directing has long been part of her "plan," ever since childhood. "It always has been since I was a kid. And then, obviously, acting took off," she said, pointing out that she also came up in the film industry when female directors were a rare commodity. "I was still growing up in a time where we didn't have Greta Gerwig—we didn't have these women who were leading by example."

Now, as in their earlier years, Saoirse affirms that it is the Gerwig effect that has shifted her own perspective and broadened her view of

FILM AWARDS
EE
EE

"I'd **love** to do that [directing] next. That was **always** a **passion** of **mine.**"

"I will stand by really wanting to play a Bond villain, which I will say again and again."

what's possible. "I think working with her had such a seismic effect on me, as she did for so many women to just go like, 'Oh, okay.' I truly believe, as most of us do, that she is already one of the greats and she will be put in the category of the Scorseses and the Coppolas, where it was only men before. Greta is already there. And so I think to work so closely with her while that was being realized by the world, suddenly made me go, 'Oh, maybe I can do this thing that I've always wanted to do.' And it's not that I think I'll be any good at it, but I feel like there's a world now where I can at least try."

As for future dream projects with Gerwig, Saoirse knows exactly what she'd want them to make. "I'm not a singer, but I would love to be in a musical," she told *The Playlist*. "I'd love to be in a film musical. I think that would be really fun. And I've decided that Greta [Gerwig] is going to write it." Was Gerwig aware of this theoretical commitment? "She will in time. That's good. I'll tell her when I'm ready."

Saoirse has also detailed other directors she's eager to work with down the line. The first comes as no surprise. "I want to work with Greta till the day I die," she told *Vanity Fair*. "We do have a very special relationship. I think her and [*Brooklyn*'s] John Crowley for me are the directors that I would love to work with again and again, because they've just made me better and better." Also on her list are a commanding and eclectically international collection of filmmakers, including Mexican filmmaker and Best Director winner for *The Shape of Water*, Guillermo del Toro ("I've always been a really huge fan of his"), Norwegian filmmaker Halfdan Ullmann Tøndel (*Armand*), Irish filmmaker Lenny Abrahamson (*Room*), and New Zealand filmmaker Jane Campion. Campion broke ground as the first woman to be awarded the Palme d'Or

Saoirse at the Variety Sundance Studio, presented by Audible, January 2024.

at Cannes, and the only woman to be twice nominated for Best Director at the Academy Awards (she won for *The Piano*).

Running parallel to her directing, producing, and writing (Saoirse revealed to *Vanity Fair* that she has a short film that she's halfway through writing, "but I need to just get up off my arse and do it.") ambitions, Saoirse has also expressed an interest in being involved in larger productions as an actor. Namely, as a Bond villain. "I will stand by really wanting to play a Bond villain, which I will say again and again," she told *Vanity Fair*, a sentiment echoed in other interviews. "Because anytime that I've gotten a chance to play someone who's a little bit evil, I just love it. And I think it would be really fun to do that again."

She has always set ever-increasing expectations for herself and risen to meet the challenge. She's a seasoned pro with a lifetime's worth of experience—yet she's still only in her early thirties, so she's also just getting started. And in her own words, she remains hungry.

When it comes to her work-life balance, Saoirse is fulfilled and more willing to share with the public. She related to *USA Today*: "My life has become so much more than just work," she explained. "For a long time, that's all I did; that's how I met people and made sense of the world." She went on, saying, "I feel like I'm part of a group, which I never thought I would have," she revealed. "I used to think, 'You'll never have friends. You'll never have a partner.' I was so in my own world, in a lot of ways. So now, to feel like I've got a very rich personal and social life—it's so precious to me."

But that's not to say she's done. To *Vanity Fair*, when it comes to her career, Saoirse claims there isn't an end-date in sight: "I will say that I've always wanted to play roles that are different from the last one that I played," she explained, "but I do feel I have so much experience now at this stage and I'm still so hungry to be pushed and challenged in the way that I always was when I was younger . . . I've never just wanted to do a job just for the sake of it."

Knowing her as we know her now, it's easy to predict that there will be glittering awards, show-stopping outfits, and warm and witty asides on the publicity circuit. It's with a great degree of certainty that we can predict impassioned championing for just causes and important work that shines attention on inequality. Saoirse Ronan is here to stay. And she'll keep doing what she's always done best—growing and changing as we watch.

Saoirse on the red carpet of the Film Independent Spirit Awards, March 2018.

"I do feel I have so much experience now at this stage and I'm still so hungry to be pushed and challenged in the way that I always was when I was younger."

Filmography

FILM

Acting

2007
I Could Never Be Your Woman (Role: Izzie Mensforth)
The Christmas Miracle of Jonathan Toomey (Role: Celia Hardwick)
Atonement (Role: Briony Tallis, aged thirteen)
Death Defying Acts (Role: Benji McGarvie)

2008
City of Ember (Role: Lina Mayfleet)

2009
The Lovely Bones (Role: Susie Salmon)

2010
The Secret World of Arrietty (Voice: Arrietty, UK [uncredited])
The Way Back (Role: Irena Zielińska)

2011
Hanna (Role: Hanna)
Violet & Daisy (Role: Daisy)

2012
Byzantium (Role: Eleanor Webb)

2013
The Host (Role: Melanie Stryder/Wanderer "Wanda")
How I Live Now (Role: Daisy)
Justin and the Knights of Valour (Voice: Talia)

Saoirse at Scotland's premiere of *Mary Queen of Scots*, January 2019.

2014

The Grand Budapest Hotel (Role: Agatha)
Muppets Most Wanted (Role: Ballerina)
Lost River (Role: Rat)

2015

Stockholm, Pennsylvania (Role: Leia Dargon)
Weepah Way for Now (Voice: Emily)
Brooklyn (Role: Eilis Lacey)

2017

Loving Vincent (Voice: Marguerite Gachet)
Lady Bird (Role: Christine "Lady Bird" McPherson)
On Chesil Beach (Role: Florence Ponting)

2018

The Seagull (Role: Nina Zarechnaya)
Mary Queen of Scots (Role: Mary Stuart)

2019

Little Women (Role: Josephine "Jo" March)

2020

Ammonite (Role: Charlotte Murchison)

2021

The French Dispatch (Role: Junkie/Showgirl #1)

2022

See How They Run (Role: Constable Stalker)

2023

Foe (Role: Henrietta)

2024

The Outrun (Role: Rona)
Blitz (Role: Rita)

TBD

Bad Apples (Role: Maria)

Deep Cuts (Role: Percy Marks)

Producing

2024

The Outrun

TBD

Deep Cuts

TELEVISION

Acting

2003

The Clinic (Role: Rhiannon Geraghty)

2005

Proof (Role: Orla Boland)

2014

Robot Chicken (Role: Various voices)

2017

Saturday Night Live (Role: Herself [host] and various characters; episode: "Saoirse Ronan/U2")

Riverdale (Role: Performer [uncredited]; episode: "Chapter One: The River's Edge")

2020

Killing Eve (Role: Performer; episode: "Are You Leading or Am I?")

STAGE

Acting

2016

The Crucible (Role: Abigail Williams at Walter Kerr Theatre, Broadway)

2021

The Tragedy of Macbeth (Role: Lady Macbeth at Almeida Theatre, West End)

Awards and Nominations

ACADEMY AWARDS

2008: Best Supporting Actress, *Atonement* (Nominated)
2016: Best Actress, *Brooklyn* (Nominated)
2018: Best Actress, *Lady Bird* (Nominated)
2020: Best Actress, *Little Women* (Nominated)

BAFTA AWARDS

2008: Best Actress in a Supporting Role, *Atonement* (Nominated)
2010: Best Actress in a Leading Role, *The Lovely Bones* (Nominated)
2016: Best Actress in a Leading Role, *Brooklyn* (Nominated)
2018: Best Actress in a Leading Role, *Lady Bird* (Nominated)
2020: Best Actress in a Leading Role, *Little Women* (Nominated)
2025: Best Actress in a Leading Role, *The Outrun* (Nominated)
2025: Outstanding British Film, *The Outrun* (Nominated)

BRITISH INDEPENDENT FILM AWARDS

2013: Best Actress, *How I Live Now* (Nominated)
2015: Best Actress, *Brooklyn* (Won)
2024: Best Lead Performance, *The Outrun* (Nominated)
2024: Best British Independent Film, *The Outrun* (Nominated)

CRITICS' CHOICE AWARDS

2008: Best Young Actress, *Atonement* (Nominated)
2010: Best Young Actor/Actress, *The Lovely Bones* (Nominated)
2010: Best Actress, *The Lovely Bones* (Nominated)
2012: Best Young Actor/Actress, *Hanna* (Nominated)
2016: Best Actress, *Brooklyn* (Nominated)

2018: Best Actress in a Comedy, *Lady Bird* (Nominated)
2018: Best Actress, *Lady Bird* (Nominated)
2020: Best Actress, *Little Women* (Nominated)

GOLDEN GLOBE AWARDS

2008: Best Supporting Actress in a Motion Picture, *Atonement* (Nominated)
2016: Best Actress in a Motion Picture in a Drama, *Brooklyn* (Nominated)
2018: Best Actress in a Motion Picture in a Musical or Comedy, *Lady Bird* (Won)
2020: Best Actress in a Motion Picture in a Drama, *Little Women* (Nominated)

INDEPENDENT SPIRIT AWARDS

2018: Best Female Lead, *Lady Bird* (Nominated)

IRISH FILM AND TELEVISION AWARDS

2008: Rising Star Award (Won)
2008: Best Actress in a Supporting Role in a Feature Film, *Atonement* (Won)
2009: Best Actress in a Supporting Role in a Film, *Death Defying Acts* (Won)
2009: Best Actress in a Lead Role in a Film, *City of Ember* (Nominated)
2010: Best Actress in a Lead Role in a Film, *The Lovely Bones* (Won)
2011: Best Actress in a Supporting Role in a Film, *The Way Back* (Won)
2012: Best Actress—Film, *Hanna* (Won)
2014: Best Lead Actress—Film, *Byzantium* (Won)
2016: Best Actress in a Lead Role—Film, *Brooklyn* (Won)
2018: Best Actress in a Lead Role—Film, *Lady Bird* (Won)
2020: Best Actress in a Lead Role—Film, *Little Women* (Nominated)
2021: Best Actress in a Supporting Role—Film, *Ammonite* (Nominated)
2024: Best Lead Actress—Film, *Foe* (Nominated)
2025: Best Supporting Actress—Film, *Blitz* (Won)
2025: Best Lead Actress—Film, *The Outrun* (Won)

SCREEN ACTORS GUILD AWARDS

2015: Outstanding Cast in a Motion Picture, *The Grand Budapest Hotel* (Nominated)
2016: Outstanding Actress in a Leading Role, *Brooklyn* (Nominated)
2018: Outstanding Actress in a Leading Role, *Lady Bird* (Nominated)
2018: Outstanding Cast in a Motion Picture, *Lady Bird* (Nominated)

Sources

Bricker, Tierney. "Inside Greta Gerwig and Saoirse Ronan's Fierce Friendship, the Hollywood Love Story We Really Need." *E! Online*, January 14, 2020. https://www.eonline.com/news/1111589/inside-greta-gerwig-and-saoirse-ronan-s-fierce-friendship-the-hollywood-love-story-we-really-need.

Brook, Charlotte. "The Many Faces of Saoirse Ronan." *Harper's Bazaar UK*, September 6, 2023. https://www.harpersbazaar.com/uk/fashion/fashion-news/a45022468/saoirse-ronan-cover-interview/.

Burroni, Christine. "Saoirse Ronan Claims She Doesn't Think She's Famous." *Page Six*, July 11, 2018. https://pagesix.com/2018/07/11/saoirse-ronan-claims-she-doesnt-think-shes-famous/.

Calkin, Jessamy. "'The New Meryl Streep': Little Women's Saoirse Ronan on Childhood Fame and the Scariest Part of Acting." *The Telegraph*, December 6, 2019. https://www.telegraph.co.uk/women/life/new-meryl-streep-little-womens-saoirse-ronan-childhood-fame/.

Crow, David. "Interview with Saoirse Ronan and Adrien Brody on The Grand Budapest Hotel." Den of Geek, March 6, 2014. https://www.denofgeek.com/movies/interview-with-saoirse-ronan-and-adrien-brody-on-the-grand-budapest-hotel/.

Dargis, Manohla. "Fighting the Peacenik Alien Within Her." *The New York Times*, March 28, 2013. https://www.nytimes.com/2013/03/29/movies/saoirse-ronan-in-the-host-from-a-stephenie-meyer-novel.html.

Downes, Philip. "Saoirse Ronan Praised After Stunning Guests Into Silence on Graham Norton Show." *Extra.ie*, October 28, 2024. https://extra.ie/2024/10/28/entertainment/saoirse-ronan-graham-norton.

Saoirse attends the world premiere of *Blitz* during the Opening Night Gala of the 68th BFI London Film Festival, October 2024.

Ebert, Roger. “After the rape and murder, the really cool part starts” RogerEbert.com, January 13, 2010. https://www.rogerebert.com/reviews/the-lovely-bones-2010.

Eddo-Lodge, Reni. “‘She’s Fascinating Eating Cornflakes’: The Endlessly Alluring Saoirse Ronan On Blitz, Kids And Marital Bliss.” *British Vogue*, October 16, 2024. https://www.vogue.co.uk/article/saoirse-ronan-british-vogue-interview.

Elmhirst, Sophie. “Saoirse Ronan: The Irish Film Star Who’s on Her Way to Broadway via Brooklyn.” *The Gentlewoman*, Autumn/Winter 2015. https://thegentlewoman.co.uk/library/saoirse-ronan.

Erbland, Kate. “Greta Gerwig Explains How Much of Her Charming Coming-of-Age Film ‘Lady Bird’ Was Inspired By Her Own Youth.” *IndieWire*, October 6, 2017. https://www.indiewire.com/features/general/greta-gerwig-lady-bird-inspired-by-youth-1201884532/.

Focus News. “Behind the Scenes of *Hanna*: Making an Action Heroine for the 21st Century.” Focus Features, February 1, 2011. https://www.focusfeatures.com/article/behind_the_scenes_of_hanna__making_an_action_heroine_for_the_2.

Ford, Rebecca. “Greta Gerwig and Saoirse Ronan Want to ‘Be Old Ladies Together Making Movies About Old Ladies.’” *The Hollywood Reporter*, January 30, 2020. https://www.hollywoodreporter.com/movies/movie-news/greta-gerwig-saoirse-ronan-what-makes-unique-collaboration-work-1273960/.

Galuppo, Mia. “Saoirse Ronan: ‘Lady Bird’ Shows ‘the Beauty and Frustration of Being a Teenager.’” *The Hollywood Reporter*, February 21, 2018. https://www.hollywoodreporter.com/news/general-news/saoirse-ronan-lady-bird-shows-beauty-frustration-being-a-teenager-1086310/.

Hayes, Martha. “From Theatrical Pedigree to an A-List Girlfriend, Jack Lowden Has All the Hallmarks of a Rising Star.” *The Standard*, February 21, 2019. https://www.standard.co.uk/lifestyle/jack-lowden-interview-a4072036.html.

Hirschberg, Lynn. "Saoirse Ronan Swears She Has A Special Connection With Alanis Morissette." *W* Magazine, January 5, 2018. https://www.wmagazine.com/story/saoirse-ronan-lady-bird-greta-gerwig-alanis-morissette.

Hyde, Marina. "I Don't Expect Stone-Cold Truths from a Chatshow, but Saoirse Ronan Delivered One." *The Guardian*, October 29, 2024. https://www.theguardian.com/commentisfree/2024/oct/29/chatshow-saoirse-ronan-graham-norton-women.

Lawler, Kelly. "Saoirse Ronan Is Wearing a Grown-Up Version of Her First Oscar Dress." *USA Today*, February 28, 2016. https://www.usatoday.com/story/life/entertainthis/2016/02/28/saoirse-ronan-oscars-academy-awards-dress-brooklyn-atonement/81086810/.

Leibert, Emily. "Saoirse Ronan Left These Famous Men Speechless." *The Cut*, October 28, 2024. https://www.thecut.com/article/saoirse-ronan-left-paul-mescal-and-eddie-redmayne-speechless.html.

Little Gold Men Podcast. "Greta Gerwig on the *Little Women* Scene Inspired by Meryl Streep." *Vanity Fair*, December 12, 2019. https://www.vanityfair.com/hollywood/2019/12/little-gold-men-podcast-greta-gerwig-interview.

Maitland, Hayley. "Saoirse Ronan and James McArdle Are Bringing an 'Apocalyptic' Take on *Macbeth* to the London Stage." *Vogue*, September 21, 2021. https://www.vogue.com/article/saoirse-ronan-james-mcardle-the-tragedy-of-macbeth-london.

Mancuso, Vinnie. "The Subtle Art of Saoirse Ronan." *Backstage*, November 7, 2024. https://www.backstage.com/magazine/article/saoirse-ronan-outrun-blitz-interview-photos-77903.

Martin, Michel, Host. "Greta Gerwig On Her 'Little Women' Film Adaptation." NPR, December 22, 2019. https://www.npr.org/2019/12/22/790631863/greta-gerwig-on-her-little-women-film-adaptation.

McGowan, Sharon. "Atonement Director Joe Wright Opens Up About Casting Saoirse Ronan in Her First Hollywood Movie." *Irish Mirror*, December 18, 2017. https://www.irishmirror.ie/showbiz/irish-showbiz/atonement-director-joe-wright-opens-11717746.

Morales, Wilson. "Hanna / Saoirse Ronan Interview." *Blackfilm*, March 27, 2011. https://www.blackfilm.com/read/hanna-saoirse-ronan-interview/.

Miller, Julie. "Saoirse Ronan Reveals the Secrets Behind Her Stunning Lady Bird Transformation." *Vanity Fair*, November 9, 2017. https://www.vanityfair.com/hollywood/2017/11/saoirse-ronan-lady-bird-in-character.

Newbold, Alice. "Saoirse Ronan's Golden Globes Versace Gown 'Is Not About Sex, It's About Strength'." *Vogue UK*, January 8, 2018. https://www.vogue.co.uk/article/saoirse-ronan-stylist-elizabeth-saltzman.

O'Dowd, Niall. "Saoirse Ronan's 'Illegal' Irish Parents and Her Start in the Bronx." *IrishCentral*, January 10, 2018. https://www.irishcentral.com/culture/entertainment/saoirse-ronan-illegal-irish-parents-bronx.

Rea, Steven. "Art Imitates Life for Actress Saoirse Ronan in 'Brooklyn.'" *The Providence Journal*, November 19, 2015. https://www.providencejournal.com/story/entertainment/movies/2015/11/20/art-imitates-life-for-actress/32978470007/.

Ronan, Saoirse, as told to Rebecca Milzoff. "Saoirse Ronan on *Brooklyn*, Broadway, and Riding the Subway." *The Cut*, February 7, 2016. https://www.thecut.com/2016/02/saoirse-ronan-on-brooklyn-and-broadway.html.

Rooney, Sally. "Saoirse Ronan on Growing Up on Camera, the Changing Politics of Ireland, and Becoming a Queen." *Vogue*, July 11, 2018. https://www.vogue.com/article/saoirse-ronan-vogue-cover-august-2018-issue.

Ryan, Patrick. "Saoirse Ronan Made a Life for Herself. Now, She's 'Ready to Be Out There Again.'" *USA Today*, October 3, 2024. https://www.usatoday.com/story/entertainment/movies/2024/10/03/saoirse-ronan-interview-outrun-blitz/75449244007/.

Santa Barbara International Film Festival Official YouTube Channel. "Saoirse Ronan Discusses Atonement & Her First Oscar Nomination." YouTube, December 7, 2007. https://www.youtube.com/watch?v=8i2Gl-vaIMv8.

Saperstein, Pat. "Greta Gerwig and Saoirse Ronan on How They Found the Voice of 'Lady Bird.'" *Variety*, January 2, 2018. https://variety.com/2018/film/features/greta-gerwig-saoirse-ronan-lady-bird-interview-collaboration-1202650197/.

Scott, A. O., and Manohla Dargis. "The 25 Greatest Actors of the 21st Century (So Far)." *The New York Times*, November 25, 2020. https://www.nytimes.com/interactive/2020/movies/greatest-actors-actresses.html.

Slankard, Jacob. "Saoirse Ronan's Performance in 'Atonement' Was So Good, It Made Us Hate a Child." *Collider*, May 5, 2024. https://collider.com/saoirse-ronan-atonement/.

Stivale, Shelby. "Saoirse Ronan and Longtime Love Jack Lowden's Low-Key Relationship Timeline." *Us Weekly*, April 2, 2023. https://www.usmagazine.com/celebrity-news/news/saoirse-ronan-and-jack-lowdens-low-key-relationship-timeline/.

Stolworthy, Jacob. "Darkest Hour Director Joe Wright Shares Candid Thoughts on Each of His Films." *Independent*, May 30, 2018. https://www.independent.co.uk/arts-entertainment/films/features/darkest-hour-joe-wright-interview-films-gary-oldman-churchill-hanna-atonement-anna-karenina-saoirse-ronan-filmography-a8149826.html.

Time Out, "Saoirse Ronan: 'I Could Have Ended Up Like Lindsay Lohan.'" May 29, 2013. https://www.timeout.com/film/saoirse-ronan-i-could-have-ended-up-like-lindsay-lohan.

Utichi, Joe. "Saoirse Ronan Lets Go Of Fears On 'Little Women', Is Ready To Follow Greta Gerwig Into Directing." *Deadline*, January 4, 2020. https://deadline.com/2020/01/saoirse-ronan-lets-go-of-fears-on-little-women-is-ready-to-follow-greta-gerwig-into-directing-1202820743/.

Vanity Fair Official YouTube Channel. "Saoirse Ronan Rewatches Little Women, Lady Bird, Atonement & More." December 12, 2023. https://www.youtube.com/watch?v=RBFpf7LRajY.

Wagner, Erica. "Saoirse Ronan on British Monarchs, Irish Borders and Mary Queen of Scots." *Harper's Bazaar UK*, January 15, 2019. https://www.harpersbazaar.com/uk/fashion/a25642449/saoirse-ronan-february-issue/.

Whipp, Glenn. "Q&A: Through 'Lady Bird,' Greta Gerwig and Saoirse Ronan Find Connections in Art and Life." *Los Angeles Times*, January 25, 2018. https://www.latimes.com/entertainment/envelope/la-en-mn-ladybird-saoirse-ronan-greta-gerwig-20180125-htmlstory.html.

Saoirse attends the Calvin Klein Collection fashion show, September 2018.

Photo Credits

PAGE 2: Rodin Eckenroth / GA / The Hollywood Reporter / Getty Images • **PAGE 4:** Amy Sussman / Getty Images • **PAGE 6:** Variety / Getty Images • **PAGE 9:** PA Images / Alamy Stock Photo • **PAGE 11:** Collection Christophel / Alamy Stock Photo • **PAGE 13:** Photo 12 / Alamy Stock Photo • **PAGE 14:** Carlo Paloni / BAFTA / Getty Images • **PAGE 17:** Rich Fury / Stringer / Getty Images • **PAGE 18:** Bauer Martinez Studios /Album / Alamy Stock Photo • **PAGE 23:** Niall Carson / PA Images / Getty Images • **PAGE 24:** Niall Carson/PA Images / Alamy Stock Photo • **PAGE 27:** Photo 12 / Alamy Stock Photo • **PAGE 29:** Photo 12 / Alamy Stock Photo • **PAGE 30:** Entertainment Pictures / Alamy Stock Photo • **PAGE 33:** WENN Rights Ltd / Alamy Stock Photo • **PAGE 34:** Entertainment Pictures / Alamy Stock Photo • **PAGE 36:** Antony Jones / Getty Images • **PAGE 39:** Moviestore Collection Ltd / Alamy Stock Photo • **PAGE 41:** Moviestore Collection Ltd / Alamy Stock Photo • **PAGE 43:** PictureLux / The Hollywood Archive / Alamy Stock Photo • **PAGE 46:** Alberto Pizzoli / Getty Images • Page 48: PictureLux / The Hollywood Archive / Alamy Stock Photo • **PAGE 51:** Marty Melville / Stringer / Getty Images • **PAGE 53:** AJ Pics / Alamy Stock Photo • **PAGE 54:** Vera Anderson / Getty Images • **PAGE 56:** Cinematic / Alamy Stock Photo • **PAGE 61:** Cinematic / Alamy Stock Photo • **PAGE 62:** Entertainment Pictures / Alamy Stock Photo • **PAGE 63:** Photo 12 / Alamy Stock Photo • **PAGE 65:** CTK / Alamy Stock Photo • **PAGE 67:** Neilson Barnard / Getty Images • **PAGE 68:** Moviestore Collection Ltd / Alamy Stock Photo • **PAGE 71:** Todd Williamson / Getty Images • **PAGE 72:** Moviestore Collection Ltd / Alamy Stock Photo • **PAGE 73:** Jeff Kravitz / FilmMagic, Inc / Getty Images • **PAGE 75:** Michael Hurcomb / Getty Images • **PAGE 77:** AJ Pics / Alamy Stock Photo • **PAGE 78:** Jesse Grant / Stringer • **PAGE 80:** Kevork Djansezian / Stringer / Getty • **PAGE 83:** Album / Alamy Stock Photo • **PAGE 84:** Photo 12 / Alamy Stock Photo • **PAGE 87:** Kevin Winter / Getty Images • **PAGE 88:** Christopher Polk / Getty Images • **PAGE 91:** Pictorial Press Ltd / Alamy Stock Photo • **PAGE 93:** Photo 12 / Alamy Stock Photo • **PAGE 95:** Photo 12 / Alamy Stock Photo • **PAGE 96:** Photo 12 / Alamy Stock Photo • **PAGE 97:** Entertainment Pictures / Alamy Stock Photo • **PAGE 98:** Photo 12

/ Alamy Stock Photo • **PAGE 100:** Album / Alamy Stock Photo • **PAGE 101:** Album / Alamy Stock Photo • **PAGE 103:** Eric Charbonneau / Getty Images • **PAGE 107:** Photo 12 / Alamy Stock Photo • **PAGE 108:** Dave Benett / Getty Images • **PAGE 111:** Stefanie Keenan / Getty Images • **PAGE 112:** Araya Doheny / Getty Images • **PAGE 114:** Kevork Djansezian/BAFTA LA / Getty Images • **PAGE 117:** Matt Winkelmeyer / Getty Images • **PAGE 119:** TCD/Prod.DB / Alamy Stock Photo • **PAGE 120:** Jason Kempin / Getty Images • **PAGE 123:** Album / Alamy Stock Photo • **PAGE 124:** Entertainment Pictures / Alamy Stock Photo • **PAGE 126:** Dave Benett / Getty Images • **PAGE 129:** Photo 12 / Alamy Stock Photo • **PAGE 130:** Walter McBride / Getty Images • **PAGE 133:** Walter McBride / Getty Images • **PAGE 134:** Dimitrios Kambouris / Getty Images • **PAGE 139:** Dave Benett / Getty Images • **PAGE 141:** BFA / Alamy Stock Photo • **PAGE 146:** Allen J. Schaben / Los Angeles Times / Getty Images • **PAGE 149:** Kurt Krieger - Corbis / Getty Images • **PAGE 151:** Vittorio Zunino Celotto /Getty Images • **PAGE 153:** Kevin Winter / Getty Images • **PAGE 154:** Christopher Polk / Getty Images • **PAGE 158:** Yui Mok - PA Images / Getty Images • **PAGE 159:** Moviestore Collection Ltd / Alamy Stock Photo • **PAGE 161:** Graham Denholm / Stringer/Getty Images • **PAGE 163:** WWD / Getty Images • **PAGE 164:** BFA / Alamy Stock Photo • **PAGE 166:** Joe Maher/BAFTA / Getty Images • **PAGE 168:** Album / Alamy Stock Photo • **PAGE 169:** Entertainment Pictures / Alamy Stock Photo • **PAGE 171:** Gilbert Flores / Contributor • **PAGE 173:** Album / Alamy Stock Photo • **PAGE 174:** Kevin Mazur / Getty Images • **PAGE 176:** FlixPix / Alamy Stock Photo • **PAGE 177:** FlixPix / Alamy Stock Photo • **PAGE 178:** BFA / Alamy Stock Photo • **PAGE 181:** Pascal Le Segretain /Getty Images • **PAGE 182:** Monica Schipper / Getty Images • **PAGE 185:** Matt Winkelmeyer / Getty Images • **PAGE 186:** Duncan McGlynn / Stringer / Getty Images • **PAGE 194:** Gareth Cattermole / Getty Images • **PAGE 201:** Monica Schipper / Stringer /Getty Images **PAGE 204:** Dave Benett / Getty Images • **PAGE 206:** Christopher Polk / Getty Images • **COVER:** Matt Winkelmeyer / Getty Images

Acknowledgments

Thank you to my mother, Jean, who taught me to appreciate stories, and to love the telling of them. Thank you to my sister, Sarra, for helping me to see so much more of the world. Thanks to the family and friends who have heard too much about this project. Many thanks to the team at Quarto and my editor, the brilliant, unflappable Katey Abraham. And thank you, Eric, for watching a never-ending stream of Saoirse Ronan movies with me, absorbing Saoirse Ronan's life history through osmosis, and for always keeping me caffeinated.

Saoirse attends the British Academy Film Awards Nominees' Party at Kensington Palace, February 2020.

About the Author

Kaila Hale-Stern is an entertainment journalist and author. She was the Movies & TV Deputy Editor at *Screen Rant* and previously served as Managing Editor of *The Mary Sue* for half a decade. There she wrote as a film and television critic, with an emphasis on the intersectionality of emerging media. She was a senior writer at *Gizmodo*, specializing in online communities, and reviewed theatrical productions for *io9*. Her byline has appeared in *New York Magazine*'s *The Cut, Cosmopolitan, Wired, Gawker, Insider,* and *The Awl*. She is also an author of historical fiction, and once helped open a magical brick-and-mortar bookstore. A native New Yorker, she lives in Brooklyn with her partner and a badly behaved cat.

Saoirse attends the 90th Annual Academy Awards, March 2018.

First published in 2026 by Epic Ink,
an imprint of The Quarto Group,
142 West 36th Street, 4th Floor,
New York, NY 10018, USA
(212) 779-4972 www.Quarto.com

EEA Representation, WTS Tax d.o.o.,
Žanova ulica 3, 4000 Kranj, Slovenia.
www.wts-tax.si

10 9 8 7 6 5 4 3 2 1

ISBN: 978-0-7603-9986-6

Digital edition published in 2026
eISBN: 978-0-7603-9987-3

Library of Congress Cataloging-in-Publication Data

Names: Hale-Stern, Kaila author
Title: Saoirse : the work, life, and style of Saoirse Ronan / Kaila Hale-Stern.
Description: New York : Epic Ink, 2026. | Series: Frame by frame | Includes bibliographical references. | Summary: "Saoirse offers a richly illustrated behind-the-scenes tour through the life and career of the beloved actress"-- Provided by publisher.
Identifiers: LCCN 2025028805 (print) | LCCN 2025028806 (ebook) | ISBN 9780760399866 | ISBN 9780760399873 ebook
Subjects: LCSH: Ronan, Saoirse, 1994- | Motion picture actors and actresses--Ireland--Biography | LCGFT: Biographies
Classification: LCC PN2601.R66 H35 2026 (print) | LCC PN2601.R66 (ebook) | DDC 791.4302/8092 [B]--dc23/eng/20250627
LC record available at https://lccn.loc.gov/2025028805
LC ebook record available at https://lccn.loc.gov/2025028806

Group Publisher: Rage Kindelsperger
Creative Director: Laura Drew
Managing Editor: Cara Donaldson
Editor: Katelynn Abraham
Cover and Interior Design: Laura Klynstra

Printed in Huizhou, Guangdong, China TT102025